KRECHINSKY'S WEDDING

KRECHINSKY'S WEDDING

A Comedy
in Three Acts

by ALEXANDER SUKHOVO-KOBYLIN

Translated by Robert Magidoff

The University of Michigan Press
Ann Arbor

Library of Congress Catalog Card No. 60-15774

Published in the United States of America by
The University of Michigan Press and simultaneously
in Toronto, Canada, by Ambassador Books Limited

Designed and illustrated by Stuart Ross

Manufactured in the United States of America by
The Haddon Craftsmen, Inc., Scranton, Pa.

KRECHINSKY'S WEDDING

A NOTE ON THE AUTHOR

A wealthy Russian nobleman, Alexander Vasilyevich Sukhovo-Kobylin, devoted most of his long life (1817-1903) to philosophical writings which were destroyed in a fire before they could be published. Sukhovo-Kobylin's fame rests solely on three plays—his entire literary output.

This trilogy was written under the tragic impact of his seven-year struggle (1850-57) to clear himself of the charge that he murdered his French mistress. In the end he was acquitted, but had to spend part of that period in prison where, in 1854, he wrote the final scenes of *Krechinsky's Wedding*. Its premiere took place the next year.

Unlike the two plays that followed (*The Affair*, completed in 1861, and *The Death of Tarelkin*, in 1868), grotesque and savage in their bitterness, *Krechinsky's Wedding* is a light fast-moving farce in which Sukhovo-Kobylin displays superb command of language and of stagecraft.

Probably the only masterpiece of pure comedy in Russian literature, this play has, for generations of theatergoers in old and new Russia, rivaled in popularity the two immortal comedies of social satire, Griboyedov's *Wit Works Woe* and Gogol's *The Inspector-General*.

In 1902 Sukhovo-Kobylin was named an honorary member of the Literature Branch of the Academy of Sciences—the highest form of recognition that could be accorded to a writer in prerevolutionary Russia.

R.M.

CHARACTERS

PIOTR KONSTANTINYCH MUROMSKY, a well-to-do landowner, about sixty years old, who lives in the country.

LIDOCHKA, his daughter.

ANNA ANTONOVNA ATUYEVA, her aunt, a middle-aged woman.

VLADIMIR DMITRICH NELKIN, a young landowner, close neighbor of the Muromsky's, who has done military service. Wears mustache.

MIKHAIL VASILICH KRECHINSKY, a well-built man with regular and striking features; bushy side whiskers but no mustache; in his late thirties.

IVAN ANTONICH RASPLUYEV, a stocky little man of about fifty.

NIKANOR SAVICH BEK, a moneylender.

SHCHEBNEV, a merchant.

FYODOR, Krechinsky's valet.

TISHKA, Muromsky's footman.

A POLICE OFFICER.

SERVANTS.

The action takes place in Moscow.

ACT I

Drawing room in the Muromsky house.
Morning. Facing the audience, a large door
opens on the front staircase; to the
right, a door leading to Muromsky's quar-
ters; to the left, a door leading to the rooms
shared by Atuyeva and Lidochka. A
table near the sofa has been set for tea.

SCENE I

ATUYEVA.   (Enters through the door on the left, inspects
the room, and opens the door to the front staircase) Tishka! Hey, Tishka!

TISHKA.   (Backstage) Co-ming! (Enters in livery, with
a wide yellow sash across his chest, unkempt
and somewhat under the influence of alcohol)*

ATUYEVA.   (Takes a long look at Tishka) What a sight
you are! (Pause) Why haven't you combed
your hair?

TISHKA.   But no, Anna Antonovna, I've combed it.

ATUYEVA.   And why haven't you washed your face?

TISHKA.   But madame, I have washed it. I certainly
washed it. From the moment you ordered me to
wash my face, I keep it washed—always.

* The author finds it necessary to point out that Tishka's condition,
although certainly reprehensible, is not the coarse state of drunkenness
which is, unfortunately, not infrequently re-created on the stage, but
rather a certain agreeableness of mood permeating his being. The mood
manifests itself in a zealous discharge of duty with, however, frequently
disheartening results; in a sing-song rhythm of speech; in a scarcely
noticeable quest for equilibrium; but above all in an unperturbable
serenity, in the face of Anna Antonovna's irascibility and sober ir-
ritability.

ATUYEVA.	Has the German brought the bell?
TISHKA.	He brought it, madame, he brought the bell.
ATUYEVA.	Let me have it, Tishka, and bring the step-ladder. (*Tishka brings the bell and the ladder*) Now, listen—Oh, what's the use—you're too dumb to understand anything.
TISHKA.	Have pity, Anna Antonovna, why shouldn't I understand? I understand everything your grace chooses to say.
ATUYEVA.	If a lady calls, ring twice.
TISHKA.	Yes, ma'am.
ATUYEVA.	If a gentleman calls, one ring.
TISHKA.	Yes, ma'am.
ATUYEVA.	If it is a lady of no importance, or just some female, don't ring at all.
TISHKA.	That can be done.
ATUYEVA.	If it's a storekeeper or a merchant of some kind, there's no need to ring, either.
TISHKA.	This, too, can be done, Anna Antonovna.
ATUYEVA.	So, you understand?
TISHKA.	Every bit of it, madame, every bit . . . Except . . . if I ring, there's no need to announce the guests?
ATUYEVA.	What do you mean, no need to announce? By all means, announce!
TISHKA.	So, first you want me to do the ringing, and then the announcing?
ATUYEVA.	Oh, what an idiot! I-di-ot! How can you, block-head, ring first, and announce afterwards?
TISHKA.	Just as you say, madame.
ATUYEVA.	Now then climb up and start hammering! (*Tishka, hammer and bell in hand, climbs the ladder*) Wait! There!
TISHKA.	(*Poising the bell*) Here?
ATUYEVA.	No, a bit higher.
TISHKA.	(*Climbing up a step*) Here?

ATUYEVA.	A bit higher, I told you.
TISHKA.	(*Raising his arm higher*) Here?
ATUYEVA.	(*Hastily*) Hold it! Hold it, I'm telling you. Lower!
TISHKA.	(*Lowering his arm*) Here?
ATUYEVA.	(*Beginning to lose her temper*) No, higher now! Lower! Higher! Lower! For Heaven's sake, Tishka. Don't you understand Russian, you fool?
TISHKA.	Begging your pardon, madame, why shouldn't I understand? I understand everything, f'course, I do.
ATUYEVA.	(*Impatiently*) What are you jabbering about?
TISHKA.	(*Removes the bell altogether and turns toward Atuyeva*) I was saying, your grace, about your saying that I don't understand Russian. But, your grace, I understand perfectly. Per-fect-ly . . .
ATUYEVA.	Are you going to fasten the bell or not?
TISHKA.	As you wish, madame.
ATUYEVA.	(*Her patience gone*) Oh! . . . Lord in Heaven! . . . You'd try the patience of an angel! You're drunk!
TISHKA.	Have a heart, your grace. I was only saying about you saying that I don't understand, but I do understand, I very well understand . . .
ATUYEVA.	(*Crossing her hands*) Trying to make a fool of me, you scoundrel? Is that why you climbed up there, to carry on a conversation? Fasten that bell, I tell you!
TISHKA.	But where, your grace?
ATUYEVA.	(*In utter fury and stamping her foot*) Any old place, you scoundrel! . . . drunken wretch! . . . You'll pay for this. Just wait! . . .
TISHKA.	(*Hastily choosing the first spot within reach, strikes at the nail with all his might*) I under-

stand . . . I completely understand, your grace
. . . ladyship . . . There! . . . there! . . . take
that! . . . Ouch! . . . (*Tumbles off stepladder;
it, too, falls*)

> *Servants come running in at the noise.*

ATUYEVA. (*Screaming*) God in Heaven! Help! He'll
break his neck!

TISHKA. (*Back on his feet, smiles*) No, madame, begging your pardon.

*The servants adjust the ladder and fasten the
bell.*

SCENE II

> *Enter Muromsky from the door on the right,
> wearing a dressing gown and smoking a pipe.*

MUROMSKY. What's all this noise about? What's going on?

ATUYEVA. Nothing at all. Tishka there is drunk again.

MUROMSKY. Drunk?

ATUYEVA. Yes! See for yourself, Piotr Konstantinych, he's
drunk as a lord.

TISHKA. Have mercy, sir, Piotr Konstantinych! Their
grace, Anna Antonovna, have deigned to say
that I'm drunk. But how? If I was drunk, how
could I fall off that monster and land on my
own two feet? I was driving the nail in, sir,
missed, and suddenly something twisted me
round and round . . .

MUROMSKY. (*Gives him a long look, shakes his head*)
Twisted you around, you say? . . . Go back to
your place, blockhead.

> *Exit Tishka, walking with extreme caution.
> The servants remove the stepladder.*

SCENE III

Muromsky and Atuyeva.

MUROMSKY. (*Watching Tishka's gait*) Drunk as an owl . . . Now, what was all that racket about?

ATUYEVA. We were fixing up a little bell.

MUROMSKY. (*Upset*) This is all we needed . . . a little bell! What for? Where? (*Catches sight of the bell*) What! Here? In the sitting room?

ATUYEVA. Yes.

MUROMSKY. But why here? To ring an alarm?

ATUYEVA. Nowadays everybody has a bell.

MUROMSKY. But it's sheer nonsense, don't you see! It's . . . it's the devil knows what it is! . . . (*Paces the floor*) Why waste words? There's no rhyme or reason in it. It'll make you bite your tongue off each time it rings! . . .

ATUYEVA. Dreaming up all sorts of nonsense! Why should I bite my tongue off? You'd better leave such things to me. I know more than you do about fixing up a house. (*Silence. Muromsky paces the floor. Atuyeva has tea*) Piotr Konstantinych, we must give a party.

MUROMSKY. (*Stops, facing Atuyeva*) A party? What kind of a party? What party are you talking about?

ATUYEVA. Come, come! As if you didn't know! Just a little ball . . . like the one we gave a few days ago.

MUROMSKY. But you told me at the time it was going to be the last. No more parties, you said.

ATUYEVA. Impossible! Utterly impossible! Convention demands it, society demands it.

MUROMSKY. How sweet of society to demand it! . . . Tell me, how, yes, just how does society, to the devil with your society, demand it? . . . Of whom? Of me, by any chance? . . . It's about time you stopped being in such a dither. Or are you out of your head?

ATUYEVA. I? . . . Out of my head? . . . I?!

MUROMSKY. Yes, you! You dragged me to Moscow—started all sorts of nonsense, fancy dress balls, spending money like water, meeting people . . . fuss and clatter! . . . You've turned my house upside down. My errand boy, Petrushka, used to be a good fellow, but the way you dressed him up he's a perfect fright. Or take that drunken fool Tishka . . . a simple cobbler, and you made him a footman! You fitted him out like a peacock, and now (*pointing to the bell*) . . . you've rigged up bells! Bells ringing like mad all over the house!

ATUYEVA. Of course, bells ringing. All the best people, I'm telling you . . .

MUROMSKY. All the best people! . . . No matter how hard you tried, you couldn't ape all their nonsense. Just look at this thing! (*Points at a vase with cards in it*) That jug! What treasures are you collecting there?

ATUYEVA. But this is for calling cards.

MUROMSKY. (*Shaking his head*) A catalogue of chatterboxes and windbags.

ATUYEVA. These visiting cards?

MUROMSKY. A list of ne'er-do-wells, tramps from every corner of the earth, who do nothing all day long, wandering from house to house, spreading dirt . . . not with their boots . . . but with their tongues.

ATUYEVA. Do you realize you are talking about the *beau monde*?

MUROMSKY. Yes! The *beau monde!*

ATUYEVA. Ha, ha, ha, it is sad and funny at the same time.

MUROMSKY.	Oh, no, just sad.
ATUYEVA.	How can you judge, Piotr Konstantinych? You don't know a thing about society.
MUROMSKY.	And I don't want to know!
ATUYEVA.	You've buried yourself in that backwood village all your life.
MUROMSKY.	Buried myself, yes. Don't complain, madame. If I hadn't buried myself, you wouldn't be giving balls.
ATUYEVA.	This is your duty, sir.
MUROMSKY.	To give balls?
ATUYEVA.	Your obligation.
MUROMSKY.	To give balls?
ATUYEVA.	You have a daughter of marriageable age.
MUROMSKY.	So, I am to call in people. (*Gesture*) This way, please! Come, one and all . . . And they, in the kindness of their hearts, will come in droves, eat us out of house and home, drink us dry, and on top of that make us a laughingstock.
ATUYEVA.	You'd rather jabber with the moujiks.
MUROMSKY.	Of course. When I talk to a moujik, either he gets something out of it, or I do. Sometimes we both do. But where is the gain in all your bell ringing?
ATUYEVA.	You can't live just for gain.
MUROMSKY.	You can't? You must!
ATUYEVA.	We are not beggars.
MUROMSKY.	We will be, the way . . . (*Throwing up his hands*) Oh, what's the use of talking to you!
ATUYEVA.	You would rather bury yourself in the backwoods and rot there with your queer characters.
MUROMSKY.	No queerer than we are, madame.
ATUYEVA.	Think again . . . The anguish those boors caused me at our last ball . . . Take that woman . . . you know the one who wore the fantastic bonnet. Fat as she is, she planted her-

self smack in the middle of the settee. Every time I looked at her, my heart sunk lower and lower.

MUROMSKY. Why, she was dressed decently. She's a good woman . . .

ATUYEVA. Who cares if she is a good woman? No one inquired about that . . . Decently dressed . . . Everyone kept asking who she was . . . I could have sunk through the floor.

MUROMSKY. No harm in people asking who she was. But let me tell you where there is harm. My daughter is a young girl and what is she being taught? What kind of talk does she hear? She never gets up before noon, and the first thing she does is to check the calling cards. There's a useful occupation for you! Then off she goes gadding about the city. In the evenings to the theater or to a ball. What kind of a life is that? What are you preparing her for? What are you teaching her? Eh? To be a flirt? To make eyes at everyone, and blabber pleasantries in French— *comment-vous portez-vous?*

ATUYEVA. And, according to you, how should she be brought up? What should she be taught?

MUROMSKY. Something useful . . . Economy. Order.

ATUYEVA. Hire a German woman to teach her that.

MUROMSKY. How to manage . . .

ATUYEVA. Hire a Finnish maid . . .

MUROMSKY. How to keep house.

ATUYEVA. Get a housekeeper! A kitchen wench for yourself!

MUROMSKY. Don't bring that up, for God's sake.

ATUYEVA. The truth hurts, doesn't it? . . . Tell me once and for all, are you giving a ball or not?

MUROMSKY. No!

ATUYEVA.	Then I shall! I'll pay for it myself. I have enough money of my own!
MUROMSKY.	Go ahead. I am not your keeper.
ATUYEVA.	Your queer notions will make Lidochka a wall-flower . . . They'll scare away eligible bachelors. All you worry about is expenses. Without expenses, my dear sir, a girl will never find a husband.
MUROMSKY.	So, without untying the purse strings, one can't marry off a girl! What rubbish! Believe me, when it is known that a girl is modest, comes from a good family, and has a dowry in the bargain, a decent man will marry her. But when you start squandering your money and putting on airs, you'll marry her off in a way you'll regret forever after.
ATUYEVA.	Would you rather give her away to some country scarecrow?
MUROMSKY.	Not a scarecrow. Somebody decent . . .
ATUYEVA.	(Interrupting him) Yes. And let that decent person bury her alive in the backwoods? Go ahead, marry her off by force . . . Bind her hand and foot . . .
MUROMSKY.	Take a breath, dear lady.
ATUYEVA.	What?
MUROMSKY.	Take a breath, I say.
ATUYEVA.	What's gotten into you?

SCENE IV

Enter Lidochka, all dressed up.

LIDOCHKA.	Good morning, papà.
MUROMSKY.	(Restored to good humor) Here she is. My lovely Lidochka. (Kisses her on the forehead) My pampered child.

LIDOCHKA	(*Kisses her aunt*) Good morning, auntie.
MUROMSKY.	What have you been doing? Whom did you dance with last night?
LIDOCHKA.	Oh, papà, I danced so much last night—so much!
ATUYEVA.	She danced the mazurka with Michel!
MUROMSKY.	Michel? You mean Mikhail Krechinsky?
LIDOCHKA.	Yes, papà.
MUROMSKY.	Good Lord! It's time he gave up that sort of thing.
ATUYEVA.	But why?
MUROMSKY.	He's getting on in years. He must be around forty.
ATUYEVA.	Where do you get that idea? He's just a trifle over thirty.
LIDOCHKA.	He's a wonderful dancer! . . . Marvelous! . . . And the way he waltzes! . . .
ATUYEVA.	And what a fine figure of a man!
MUROMSKY.	I wonder what you see in this Krechinsky. All right, he's good-looking . . . well, and likeable enough. But he's quite a gambler, I'm told.
ATUYEVA.	For Heaven's sake! You don't have to swallow everything you hear. It must be that Nelkin whispering in your ear again. But where does he hear these things? Where does he spend his time? Anyway, who doesn't play cards these days? Everybody does.
MUROMSKY.	There's more than one way of playing cards. As for Nelkin, he never goes near them.
ATUYEVA.	You and your Nelkin! You'd change your mind about him if you saw him in society. He is positively a disgrace! Why, only yesterday I got him an invitation from the countess. I dragged him to the ball—and what do you think? He slunk into a corner and crouched there, peering

at everyone like a wild animal. This is what comes of living in the country all the time.

MUROMSKY.   No harm in that. He is shy, hasn't mixed with people much. This is no vice.

ATUYEVA.   No vice, true enough. But he will never be accepted in high society. And he *will* insist on grabbing Lidochka for the waltz. He's a horrible dancer, liable to stumble and drag her down with him. The shame!

MUROMSKY.   (*Flaring up*) You're aiming too high. Make sure you don't stumble and drag Lidochka down with you.

ATUYEVA.   Not I, never.

MUROMSKY.   (*Leaving the stage*) Make sure you don't come a cropper, with all of your high society looking on.

ATUYEVA.   I won't come a cropper!

MUROMSKY.   You'd better make sure. (*Exit Muromsky*)

ATUYEVA.   Never! Never!

SCENE V

Lidochka and Atuyeva

LIDOCHKA.   Auntie, why do you make papà angry all the time?

ATUYEVA.   He tries my patience beyond words. What in the world does he see in that Nelkin? (*Pause*) Lidochka, what did you and Krechinsky talk about while you were dancing? There was something about the way you talked . . .

LIDOCHKA.   (*Hesitantly*) Nothing much, auntie.

ATUYEVA.   Were you speaking French?

LIDOCHKA.   Yes, French.

ATUYEVA.   I could die listening to French! My French is

so-so . . . but I adore, simply adore listening to it. And you, *ma chère,* are probably quite fluent?

LIDOCHKA. Quite fluent, auntie.

ATUYEVA. And Krechinsky . . . our Michel . . . does he have a good accent?

LIDOCHKA. Yes, very good.

ATUYEVA. It sounds so clever when he talks French. He speaks so quickly, the words just pour out. And that word he always uses . . . what is it? Oh, yes, *parbleu!* The way he says it! How is it you never say *parbleu?*

LIDOCHKA. But no, auntie, I do say it sometimes.

ATUYEVA. Fine! But why do you look so sad, so *triste?*

LIDOCHKA. Oh, auntie . . . I honestly don't know how to put it . . .

ATUYEVA. Put what, my sweet?

LIDOCHKA. Auntie! He proposed to me last night.

ATUYEVA. Who? Michel? Really? How did he say it?

LIDOCHKA. I'm too embarrassed to repeat it, auntie . . . He said that he loved me . . . oh, so much! . . .

ATUYEVA. And you? What did you say?

LIDOCHKA. I couldn't say anything. I only said: "Do you really love me?"

ATUYEVA. What else did you say?

LIDOCHKA. I couldn't say anything else.

ATUYEVA. Now I understand why you kept twisting the ribbon in your hands. I watched you. Well . . . you mean to say that was really all you said to him? Didn't I teach you what to say?

LIDOCHKA. Yes, auntie. I told him—*parlez à ma tante et à papa.*

ATUYEVA. Good girl. You behaved very properly, Lidochka.

LIDOCHKA. (*After a pause*) Oh, auntie, I feel like crying.

ATUYEVA. Why would you want to cry? Don't you like him?

LIDOCHKA. I do, I do! I like him very much. (*Throws her-*

	self on her aunt's neck and bursts out crying) Dear, dear auntie . . . I am in love with him!
ATUYEVA.	Enough, Lidochka. (*Wipes Lidochka's tears with a pocket handkerchief*) No reason to cry. He is a wonderful man . . . accepted in the best society . . . He knows everybody.
LIDOCHKA.	Yes, auntie, he knows everybody. He knows everybody at all the parties. Only . . . only I am afraid of papà. He does not like Michel. He wants me to marry Nelkin.
ATUYEVA.	That's sheer nonsense, my dear. Your father wants you to marry Nelkin because he lives in the country and his estate is next to ours, furrow to furrow, as he says. That's why he wants you to marry Nelkin.
LIDOCHKA.	Papà says that Nelkin is a good man.
ATUYEVA.	Of course, he is. That's the way of the world: If a man is stupid, he is good; if he is toothless, he wags his tail. But if you marry Krechinsky . . . Michel . . . he'll set up house in grand style. You'll move in brilliant circles! He has such impeccable taste . . .
LIDOCHKA.	Yes, auntie, impeccable.
ATUYEVA.	And your diamond solitaire! How beautifully he had it set! The thing was lying in your father's strongbox for ages, but now everyone is raving about it. I'll talk to your father about Michel.
LIDOCHKA.	Auntie, Michel told me that he has to take a trip.
ATUYEVA.	Soon?
LIDOCHKA.	In a few days.
ATUYEVA.	Will he be gone long?
LIDOCHKA.	I don't know, auntie.
ATUYEVA.	That means we must give him an answer.
LIDOCHKA.	(*Sighing*) Yes, we must.

ATUYEVA.	I'll talk to your father. Right away.
LIDOCHKA.	Auntie, wouldn't it be better if Michel talked to him? You know how clever he is, how brilliant, charming . . .
ATUYEVA.	(*Taking offense*) Suit yourself. After all, I'm not your mother.
LIDOCHKA.	Oh, auntie, how can you? You are mother to me . . . sister . . . you are everything to me! You know how I love him . . . (*kisses her*) how I love him . . . (*Pause*) There is so much in that word—"love" . . .
ATUYEVA.	Now, now.
LIDOCHKA.	I don't know what's happening to me . . . My heart beats and beats, and then, suddenly, it seems to stand still. I don't understand it.
ATUYEVA.	It will pass, my dear . . . it will pass away . . . Shush, your father is coming. We'll talk to him, right here and now.

SCENE VI

Enter Muromsky

MUROMSKY.	What are you up to? Your Krechinsky is dragging me to the races today. What'll I do there? Race horses mean nothing to me.
ATUYEVA.	What difference does it make? There'll be lots of people there.
MUROMSKY.	What do you mean "people"? We're going to look at horses, not people.
ATUYEVA.	That shows how much you know about it. The entire *beau monde* will be there.
MUROMSKY.	To the devil with your *beau* . . . (*A vigorous ring of the bell*) Damnation! I won't stand for it! I'll get hold of Tishka and break his arm! My

patience is at an end! (*Pointing at the bell*) Have the goodness to get rid of it right away!

ATUYEVA.   Impossible! It's your house, but you have to keep the bell. The best homes have them.

MUROMSKY.   (*At the top of his voice*) What's got into you? I don't want bells ringing over my head, and that's all there's to it!

ATUYEVA.   Do you have to shout? God in Heaven! (*Pointing to the door and lowering her voice*) Control yourself at least in front of strangers.

SCENE VII

Nelkin enters, bows to the ladies.
Shakes hands with Muromsky.

MUROMSKY.   Nelkin, my good friend! Where have you been hiding? I've missed you.

NELKIN.   True, true, my friend . . . I'm going to the dogs. One long round of balls and parties. (*Looks up at the door*) Quite a bell you have there, madame . . . Rather piercing.

MUROMSKY.   There! I am not the only one.

NELKIN.   But let me tell you. Last night I was at a ball given by a countess and (*points at the bell*) the same thing there. I had just started up the stairs . . . everything lit up as bright as day . . . I didn't know my way around the house . . . swarms of servants, and all in livery. Well, as I was saying, I had just started up the stairs and was just getting my bearings when the bell clanged right over my head! It threw me into a cold sweat! I can hardly remember how my legs propelled me into the drawing room.

ATUYEVA.   But they did propel you in grand style!

MUROMSKY.	I'm telling you, Anna, your bells will drive me out of my own home.
NELKIN.	(*To Muromsky*) Are you about ready to leave for the country?
ATUYEVA.	We are not even thinking of the country, Monsieur Nelkin. At least, not until after Shrovetide. Nothing to do there until then.
MUROMSKY.	There she goes again! Nothing to do in the country! There's no reasoning with them! Don't you understand, madame, I must give orders to prepare for the summer. It's time to spread the manure. Without manure you won't be giving dances.
ATUYEVA.	But you have a manager on the estate. He can see to the manure.
MUROMSKY.	No, he cannot.
ATUYEVA.	It makes no sense to me . . . Do you mean to say that the landlord himself has to spread manure? . . .
MUROMSKY.	Exactly!
ATUYEVA.	A delightful occupation.
MUROMSKY.	That's where many an estate has gone to ruin . . .
ATUYEVA.	(*Interrupting*) Because of manure?
MUROMSKY.	Yes. Because of manure.
ATUYEVA.	Ha-ha-ha! My dear, don't say such things to other people. You'll be the laughingstock of Moscow.
MUROMSKY.	I don't care two pins what . . . (*Bell clangs again. Everyone in the room gives a start. Muromsky jumps up. Shouts*) Ai! Ai! God in Heaven! This will drive me insane! I can't stand it any longer! (*Walks up to Atuyeva*) Do you understand: I can't stand it any longer! Or do you want to drive me to the grave?

SCENE VIII

Enter Krechinsky—in a boisterous manner, foppishly dressed, with a cane, yellow gloves, patent-leather shoes, worn at the time for morning visits.

KRECHINSKY. Good morning, Piotr Konstantinych! (*Bows to the ladies*) Mesdames! (*Walks up to them and kisses their hands*)

NELKIN. (*Withdraws. Aside*) Up with the birds and flies straight here. (*Watching Krechinsky tell a gay story, laughing, gesticulating*) A clown! Nothing but a clown! Still, I must admit . . . He's entertaining . . . a real lady-killer . . . (*The women laugh*) There they go! Oh, women, what does it take to please you? It takes yellow gloves, patent-leather shoes, bushy side whiskers, and a lot of clatter! (*Krechinsky goes to a corner, puts down his hat and cane, takes off his gloves and silently exchanges a bow with Nelkin. Rejoins the ladies*) Oh, Lydia . . . Lydia . . .

KRECHINSKY. (*Pointing to the bell*) Ma chère madame, what is that . . . a town-meeting bell?

ATUYEVA. (*Timidly*) Town-meeting? Why town-meeting?

KRECHINSKY. A bit deafening.

MUROMSKY. (*Seizes Krechinsky's hand*) Thank you, thank you, Mikhail Vasilich, from the bottom of my heart! Thank you! (*To Atuyeva*) Madame, what do you have to say now? I knew you were over-doing it.

KRECHINSKY. What's this all about?

MUROMSKY. What a question! It's the devil's own work. Made a sick man of me. Precisely—a town-meeting bell! You'd think this was a town hall!

KRECHINSKY.	(*Walks up to the bell. Everyone follows*) Yes, quite large . . . Much too large. It has a spring, I see, a marteau. I know that kind.
NELKIN.	(*Aside*) Who but you should know about bells? That's right in your line.
ATUYEVA.	A German made it for me.
KRECHINSKY.	Yes, of course, it's a fine bell, but it should be down there, near the front door.
MUROMSKY.	Another load off my shoulders. (*Opens the door leading to the staircase*) Hey, you, Tishka! Good-for-nothing bell-ringer! (*Enter Tishka*) Take that hellish thing out of here. (*Tishka unfastens the bell, carries it away*)
KRECHINSKY.	(*To Lidochka, with a touch of familiarity*) Have you rested well after the ball, *ma chère amie*?
LIDOCHKA.	I have a slight headache.
KRECHINSKY.	What a wonderfully gay time we had!
LIDOCHKA.	Oh, yes, wonderfully gay.
KRECHINSKY.	(*To Muromsky, glibly*) Your daughter was very pretty last night . . . so fresh, so charming . . . People couldn't stop looking at her.
LIDOCHKA.	(*Rather embarrassed*) Tread softly, Mikhail Vasilich. You are praising yourself a little, you know.
MUROMSKY.	What do you mean? Praising himself? . . .
LIDOCHKA.	Of course, father. He gave me the idea for the dress and all the accessories. Auntie and I consulted him.
MUROMSKY.	Is that so? Well, live and learn! Where did you get it all—master of every trade and trifle?
KRECHINSKY.	Can't help it, sir. God's gift. And now, may I invite you into the courtyard to judge my talents along other lines (*takes him by the arm*)?
MUROMSKY.	To the courtyard? But why?
KRECHINSKY.	(*Playfully*) Have you forgotten?

MUROMSKY.	I really don't know.
KRECHINSKY.	But I do. I might fritter away my time on ball-room dresses, but I remember. The bullock?
MUROMSKY.	Oh, yes, yes, the bullock! Of course. Did you bring him in from the country?
KRECHINSKY.	Yes, he's here. He has been kicking up a dust in your yard for the past half hour.
MUROMSKY.	(*Takes his hat*) I'm curious to see it. Very curious.
KRECHINSKY.	*Mesdames*, we shall not be long. (*Takes Muromsky's arm familiarly and escorts him out*)

SCENE IX

Atuyeva, Lidochka, Nelkin

ATUYEVA.	There, Mr. Nelkin, is a real man of the world for you. *Charmant, charmant.*
NELKIN.	Yes, he is—how should I put it?—a smooth fellow, a gay bird . . . But one hears very little good about him.
ATUYEVA.	Where does one hear? Through what peephole?
NELKIN.	They say he is a desperate gambler.
ATUYEVA.	(*With vexation*) I am tired of hearing your tales, if you will excuse my saying so. All one ever hears from you is gossip, sheer gossip. After all, you don't know Moscow. Whatever you happen to hear from the first chance person, you spread all over town. No, sir, such conduct is not permissible in a large city. You are young and must be more careful of what you say, more discriminating of the company you keep. Just tell me, who was that you were sitting with at the theater the other night? Who was he?
NELKIN.	Oh, just someone I know. A local merchant.

ATUYEVA.   A merchant? Since when are you keeping company with merchants?

NELKIN.   For pity's sake! He is a well-established merchant. What a house he has!

ATUYEVA.   So, he has a house. Anyone can have a house. Since when are merchants fit company for you? And in public, at that! If any society people ever see you with him, they will stop inviting you to their homes.

NELKIN.   I am not exactly chasing after invitations.

LIDOCHKA.   (*With heat*) What are you trying to say? Who is chasing after invitations?

NELKIN.   Lidya Petrovna! Forgive me. I didn't say it with any intent, I assure you. I did not mean to imply anything.

ATUYEVA.   Enough about it! May God forgive you, young man. But you had better stop saying bad things about others. The world is full of evil talk. If you are good-looking, they say you are stupid beyond belief. If you are rich, they say you are ugly. If you are clever, they brand you a scoundrel, or something even more colorful. That's the way of the world. Let God be their judge. A man is what he is.

SCENE X

Enter Krechinsky and Muromsky.

MUROMSKY.   You're too kind, Mikhail Vasilich! (*Shakes Krechinsky's hand*) Thank you, thank you! But really . . . my conscience does not allow me . . .

KRECHINSKY. No more about it, please.

MUROMSKY.   Still, my conscience bothers me . . . I don't deserve it . . . Lida! Lidochka!

LIDOCHKA.   What is it, papà?

MUROMSKY.	You see, Krechinsky has made me a present of that bullock.
LIDOCHKA.	(*Puts her head on Muromsky's shoulder*) Is it pretty, papà?
MUROMSKY.	(*Shutting his eyes in ecstasy*) Magnificent! Just imagine! The head! The eyes! The muzzle! And the horns! (*Shutting his eyes again*) Magnificent! (*To Krechinsky*) And it's from your own estate?
KRECHINSKY.	Yes, from my estate in Simbirsk.
MUROMSKY.	So, you have an estate in Simbirsk?
KRECHINSKY.	Yes, an estate.
MUROMSKY.	With a good cattle farm?
KRECHINSKY.	A first-class cattle farm.
MUROMSKY.	Do you like cattle?
KRECHINSKY.	Very much so!
MUROMSKY.	And you also like, well . . . crops, fields, manure . . . ?
KRECHINSKY.	(With a short laugh) Also crops, fields, manure.
MUROMSKY.	But you don't seem to care for country life.
KRECHINSKY.	(*Heatedly*) Who told you that? Why, I worship the country. In the summer the countryside is a paradise. Fresh air, peace, tranquility. I walk into the orchard, the woods, the fields . . . I'm master of everything. Everything is mine. Even the blue horizon in the distance—that, too, is mine. It's magic!
MUROMSKY.	Just the way I feel.
KRECHINSKY.	I wake up early and head straight for the fields. The fields are full of warm air and sweet scents . . . Then, to the stables, the greenhouses, the vegetable garden . . .
MUROMSKY.	And the threshing floor . . .
KRECHINSKY.	And the threshing floor! Everything quivers with activity. Quiet, peaceful activity.
MUROMSKY.	Yes, quiet, peaceful activity. There, Anna, is a sensible person talking.

KRECHINSKY.   The day's job done, you've worked up an appetite, and home you go. But here you begin to miss something. Something is lacking, Piotr Konstantinych . . . Can you guess what?

MUROMSKY.   (*Gaily*) Tea. Of course, tea.

KRECHINSKY.   No, not tea. Something you need far more than tea. Something of a higher order than tea.

MUROMSKY.   (*Puzzled*) I don't know what it could be.

KRECHINSKY.   How can you say you don't know? You, of all people . . .

MUROMSKY.   I honestly don't know.

KRECHINSKY.   Why, a wife! You need a wife!

MUROMSKY.   (*With enthusiasm*) Of course, of course! A wife!

KRECHINSKY.   (*Continuing in the same vein*) And what kind of a wife? (*Looks at Lidochka*) Shapely, fair-haired, a gentle mistress of your home, with never an angry word. You come in, take her head in your hands, kiss her on both cheeks. Greetings, wife, you say, what about some tea?

ATUYEVA.   *Mon Dieu!* With such gentle manners he won't ruffle a hair on her head.

KRECHINSKY.   Oh, no, Anna Antonovna, wives don't mind their husbands ruffling their hair. It is when husbands don't—that's when wives are offended. (*Muromsky laughs. Krechinsky continuing in the same vein*) But the samovar is already boiling. Then, behold, the aged father comes in. He is as gray as an old eagle and supports himself on a crutch. He blesses your wife. And then, behold, the mischievous little grandson climbs on his knee. The boy is afraid of his mother, but clings to his grandfather. This is what I call life! (*Turns to Lidochka*) And you? Do you like the countryside?

LIDOCHKA.	I adore the countryside.
ATUYEVA.	Since when?
LIDOCHKA.	Yes, auntie, I just love the country. (*To Krechinsky*) I am very fond of pigeons, Mikhail Vasilich. I feed them myself.
KRECHINSKY.	And do you like flowers?
LIDOCHKA.	I love flowers, too.
ATUYEVA.	Oh, merciful creator! Now she loves everything!
KRECHINSKY.	I'm afraid I've let my tongue run away with me. (*Looks at his watch. To Muromsky*) It's already one o'clock. Time to go, or we'll be late. It would be wise to dress up. Half the world will be there.
MUROMSKY.	(*In a good mood*) Why not? Maybe we'll show what stuff country people are made of! It's hard to refuse such a gracious man.
LIDOCHKA.	(*Running up to her father*) Yes, yes, get all dressed up, papà! Stop pretending you are an old man. My little angel . . . (*Kisses him*) I'll go with you . . . My dear papà . . . (*kisses him again*)
KRECHINSKY.	Bravo, Lidochka, bravo! Take him in hand . . . Don't let him pretend any more . . .
MUROMSKY.	(*Laughing and caressing his daughter*) Who is pretending? More of your pranks, eh? (*Exit Muromsky and Lidochka. Nelkin follows them*)

SCENE XI

Atuyeva and Krechinsky

KRECHINSKY.	(*Looks around*) And how did you like my picture of rural life, Anna Antonovna?
ATUYEVA.	Do you really like the countryside?

KRECHINSKY.   I? The countryside? God forbid! I was only pretending.

ATUYEVA.   Why pretending?

KRECHINSKY.   No harm in amusing an old man.

ATUYEVA.   Yes, it does please him when someone praises
country life.

KRECHINSKY.   There you are! But I'd like you, Anna Antonovna, to know the real purpose behind my
words.

ATUYEVA.   What is the real purpose?

KRECHINSKY.   Madame! Anna! My friend! Who could fail to
hold you in esteem? Who could fail to appreci-
ate the way you have brought up Lidochka?

ATUYEVA.   And yet, would you believe it, her father always finds fault with me.

KRECHINSKY.   But, Anna Antonovna, you must forgive an old
man. He is a man of the soil, and such people
can see no farther than their cattle sheds and
dung hills.

ATUYEVA.   That's true. Only this morning he kept harping
about people who come to ruin because they
pay no attention to their manure.

KRECHINSKY.   Exactly! That's all they know! But you, Madame, you have established an exquisite house.
It has everything, everything—except one de-
tail: a man! Bring a man into your house, a man
of the world, clever, *comme il faut,* and your
house will be the finest in the whole city.

ATUYEVA.   That's exactly what I think.

KRECHINSKY.   I have spent many years in society, and I
know life. Real happiness lies in finding a well-
brought-up young girl, and sharing everything
with her. Anna Antonovna . . . I beg of you . . .
Give me this happiness . . . My fate is in your
hands . . .

ATUYEVA.	(*Affectedly*) How can that be? I don't understand you.
KRECHINSKY.	I ask the hand of your niece Lydia.
ATUYEVA.	Lidochka's happiness means more to me than anything else in the world. I am sure she'll be happy with you.
KRECHINSKY.	(*Kissing her hand*) Anna Antonovna! I'm so grateful!
ATUYEVA.	Have you spoken to her father?
KRECHINSKY.	Not yet.
ATUYEVA.	You must obtain his consent.
KRECHINSKY.	I know, I know. (*Aside*) That's the millstone round my neck.
ATUYEVA.	What did you say?
KRECHINSKY.	I was saying that a parent's blessing is . . . how should I put it . . . the keystone of all things.
ATUYEVA.	The very truth.
KRECHINSKY.	Then what shall we do about him?
ATUYEVA.	I am in a quandary about it myself.
KRECHINSKY.	I have it! Now, I think, is the right moment. I'll rush off to the races immediately. Society is waiting for me there. I have a big bet on with Prince Belsky. While I am gone, you detain the old man, engage him in conversation. Tell him I was in a hurry, afraid of being late, with everybody waiting for me there. And while you are at it, tell him about my proposal. (*Takes his hat*)
ATUYEVA.	Very well. I'll do it.
KRECHINSKY.	(*Kisses her hand*) Goodbye. My fate is in your hands.
ATUYEVA.	You can be sure I'll arrange everything. Good luck! (*Exit*)

SCENE XII

Krechinsky alone, then Nelkin

KRECHINSKY. (*Soliloquy*) What a trick to pull off! A cool million as good as in my hand! A million! What power! (*Pause*) To force the issue or not to force it—that is the question. An abyss, a bottomless abyss. Winner take all! The law of probability —nothing more. And what are the probabilities here? The odds against me: One—papa. A blockhead, but he sticks to fundamentals. Two —Nelkin. Well, he's neither fish nor fowl nor good red herring. The odds in my favor? One— that town-meeting bell. Two—Lidochka. Three? Oh, yes, my little bull. A strong card! Excellent moral effect. (*Nelkin enters from a side door, stops. Not noticed by Krechinsky, who is putting on his hat*) So two points against me to three in my favor. Hm . . . Yes. I'll be a married man, it seems. Everything points to a wedding. Krechinsky's wedding. (*Exit*)

NELKIN. (*In astonishment*) Krechinsky's wedding! Merciful Father! Who is the girl? Lydia . . . Lidochka . . . Oh, no! The apple is sweet but isn't meant for you . . . And yet, he threw out a feeler just a few minutes ago. A wife, he said, a wife is needed. And the devil knows what else he said. He is sharp, witty, a daredevil, damn him! But no! The old man is a match for you. You can't sweep him off his feet—he's rooted as firm as an oak. And I am here, to help out. You'll find us too much even for you! While you're showing off at the front door with your prancing ponies . . . we'll be looking in the back door. You city slickers all put up false fronts. Just wait, I'll smoke you out. There are things you're trying to cover up. I've heard at the club . . .

MUROMSKY. (*Off stage*) I'm almost ready. Coming, coming.

NELKIN. I'll get to the bottom of it all. Then I'll go straight to the old man, and say: Why don't you use your eyes, sir? You'd better watch out. (*Exit*)

SCENE XIII

Enter Muromsky, in tails, hat in hand.
Followed by Atuyeva.

MUROMSKY. Here I am, Krechinsky! (*Looks around*) But where is he?

ATUYEVA. He's gone. He said he was late, so he left in a great hurry.

MUROMSKY. Did he go to the races?

ATUYEVA. Yes, to the races. Everyone there was waiting for him—the horses, the club members. He has made a big bet with some prince.

MUROMSKY. I'll find him there.

ATUYEVA. I'd like a word with you. Please stay.

MUROMSKY. Now you say stay! Are you playing games with me? First, you say go; now—don't go.

ATUYEVA. I have a matter to discuss with you.

MUROMSKY. What matter? Some more trivialities, I suppose.

ATUYEVA. That's for you to decide. Put your hat down. I've just had a long talk with Michel . . . I mean Krechinsky.

MUROMSKY. You have been having long talks with him every day—there seems to be no end to them.

ATUYEVA. You are very much mistaken. I'm surprised you don't understand.

MUROMSKY.   Damned if I do.

ATUYEVA.   The man has been coming here every day . . . a wonderful person . . . a man of the world . . . with brilliant connections . . .

MUROMSKY.   He's welcome to them!

ATUYEVA.   Sir, you have a daughter.

MUROMSKY.   (*Looking at the ceiling*) I've known this for twenty years. Who should know it better than I?

ATUYEVA.   And you still don't understand?

MUROMSKY.   I still don't understand.

ATUYEVA.   God have mercy!

MUROMSKY.   (*Suddenly alert*) What is going on? Is he proposing marriage?

ATUYEVA.   Suppose he is? Not a bad match for Lidochka.

MUROMSKY.   He's getting on in years.

ATUYEVA.   He's no babe in the woods, if that's what you mean.

MUROMSKY.   Lidochka would never marry him.

ATUYEVA.   If she refuses, we won't force her. But suppose she accepts him? What will you say then?

MUROMSKY.   Who? I?

ATUYEVA.   Yes, you.

MUROMSKY.   I'll say . . . (*Pause. Looks at her, then rapidly*) Gobbledegook!

ATUYEVA.   What is gobbledegook?

MUROMSKY.   Stuff and nonsense, Madame!

ATUYEVA.   It's not stuff and nonsense. I am asking you a sensible question.

MUROMSKY.   If you want a sensible answer, give me time for some sensible thinking.

ATUYEVA.   What is there to think about? Thinking will not get your daughter a husband.

MUROMSKY.   What do you want me to do? Shut my eyes and throw her into the arms of the first man who happens to come along? I have to know who he is, his circumstances . . .

ATUYEVA.	Ask him for his birth certificate . . .
MUROMSKY.	I am not interested in his birth certificate. I must know . . .
ATUYEVA.	What must you know? He's been coming to the house all winter. What else do you need? Everything is crystal clear. He's accepted everywhere . . . He moves in the best circles . . . He's on intimate terms with princes and counts.
MUROMSKY.	How much property does he have?
ATUYEVA.	Only a few minutes ago he told you about his estate in Simbirsk. And he gave you that bull.
MUROMSKY.	What kind of an estate does he have? There are estates and estates.
ATUYEVA.	Anyone in his right mind can see it's a good estate. All society is waiting for him at the races. No one would be waiting if it were a miserable little estate.
MUROMSKY.	This is what *you* say.
ATUYEVA.	Then what do *you* say?
MUROMSKY.	I say what kind of an estate does he have?
ATUYEVA.	Stop pestering me!
MUROMSKY.	You are pestering me!
ATUYEVA.	Don't shout at me! I am not deaf. What is it you want, Piotr Konstantinych? Is it money you want? Hasn't Lidochka enough of her own? You are money-mad. You keep hoarding—and still not enough. What matters is—is he a good man?
MUROMSKY.	But is he a good man?
ATUYEVA.	A fine man, a wonderful man.
MUROMSKY.	People say that this wonderful man of yours gambles, hangs around the clubs, owes money.
ATUYEVA.	Who doesn't?
MUROMSKY.	A man who owes money is no son-in-law of mine.
ATUYEVA.	Then you'll have to look for a son-in-law yourself.
MUROMSKY.	I shall, if it comes to that.

ATUYEVA.   You can expect no help from me.

MUROMSKY.   I'll manage somehow.

ATUYEVA.   And let your daughter become an old maid?

MUROMSKY.   So, she'll be an old maid . . . But I am not going
               to marry her off to a goat.

ATUYEVA.   A goat? Mikhail Vasilich Krechinsky—a goat?

MUROMSKY.   Take a breath, Madame.

ATUYEVA.   What?

MUROMSKY.   Take a deep breath, I say.

ATUYEVA.   I won't stand for this! . . . Are you trying to
               make a fool of me? You don't know what to say.
               That's all there is to it.

MUROMSKY.   I don't know what to say? Is that it? Then let me
               tell you. You like him and Lidochka likes him,
               but I do not like him, and I won't let him
               marry my daughter.

ATUYEVA.   (Heatedly) You should have said so in the first
               place. Because of your whim, your daughter is
               to be unhappy for the rest of her life! And you
               call yourself a father! You are nothing but a
               tyrant!

MUROMSKY.   Who is a tyrant? I? I—a tyrant?

ATUYEVA.   (Just as heatedly) Yes, you! you!

MUROMSKY.   No, you!

ATUYEVA.   (Pointing her finger at him) You, I say.

MUROMSKY.   (Pointing his finger at her) No, you!

ATUYEVA.   You! you! you! Stop shaking your finger at me.

SCENE XIV

Enter Lidochka

LIDOCHKA.   (Runs in) Auntie! Auntie!

ATUYEVA.   (Still in a fury) I've lost all patience. It's up to
               you from now on.

LIDOCHKA.   What is it, papà?

MUROMSKY.	Nothing, my darling . . . I was just having a talk with your aunt.
ATUYEVA.	(*With renewed anger*) Darling! Darling! You had better tell your darling the things you've just been saying to me. Why are you so quiet all of a sudden?
MUROMSKY.	Why all of a sudden? I've been quiet all along.
LIDOCHKA.	Auntie, dear . . . Please, please! I beg you!
ATUYEVA.	Stop trying to calm me down! I'm no fool. Well, why are you standing there so quiet, sir? Why don't you ask her? He'll be expecting a reply. (*Lidochka eyes them both and begins to cry*)
MUROMSKY.	Very well, I'll ask her. Tell me, Lidochka, would you marry against my will?
LIDOCHKA.	Papà . . . I . . . I . . . No . . . never, never! (*Embraces Atuyeva*) You see, auntie? (*Tears in her voice*) I'll go into a convent . . . to my grandmother . . . I'll be happier there . . . (*Weeps*)
MUROMSKY.	God in Heaven! Why into a convent? Don't say such things. Don't cry. Give us time to think it over. It's all so unexpected . . .

SCENE XV

Enter Krechinsky

MUROMSKY.	Oh, my God! He's back!
KRECHINSKY.	(*Glibly*) Yes, dear sir, we have missed the races today. (*Stops. Lidochka and Muromsky are engaged in a whispered conversation. To Atuyeva*) What happened?
ATUYEVA.	He keeps saying he wants time to think it over.
KRECHINSKY.	And you lost your temper?
ATUYEVA.	(*Straightening her bonnet*) No, not a bit.
KRECHINSKY.	(*To Muromsky*) Piotr Konstantinych, please tell me what's wrong. (*Pause*) Allow me to be

36

frank. It's always better that way. I am a straightforward person. The matter will be cleared up and no grudges held. After all, you are the judge, and the verdict is yours.

MUROMSKY. We were just having a private talk among ourselves . . . about other things.

KRECHINSKY. (*Looks at them all*) Other things . . . I doubt it. I don't believe it. Needless detours will get us nowhere. Permit me to come straight to the point. Last night I proposed to your daughter. I've just had a talk with her aunt. And now I am here, your obedient servant.

MUROMSKY. But this is no trifling matter. In a matter so important I must ask you to give us a little time to think it over.

KRECHINSKY. There has been plenty of time, I thought.

MUROMSKY. I have only just now heard about it.

KRECHINSKY. I don't mean that. I have been frequenting your home for several months now. This should have given you enough time to think . . .

MUROMSKY. But it never entered my head.

KRECHINSKY. Then the fault is yours, not mine. How could you have failed to think about it? You know that no gentleman would risk compromising a young lady by frequenting her home unless he had some special reason.

MUROMSKY. Yes, of course.

KRECHINSKY. May I, therefore, ask you not to postpone your decision? As I've told your daughter, I must go off on a journey soon.

MUROMSKY. (*Undecided*) What shall I say? God's truth, I don't know.

KRECHINSKY. What is troubling you? My circumstances?

MUROMSKY. Yes, your circumstances, too.

KRECHINSKY. My circumstances are an open book. My style of living speaks for itself. I'm not like you—I don't inquire about your daughter's dowry.

MUROMSKY.	What is there to inquire? She's all I have.
KRECHINSKY.	And I am all *I* have.
MUROMSKY.	So far so good. But in matters of this sort a concreteness is needed, if I may say so.
KRECHINSKY.	Concreteness? Well, here is something concrete. I have enough of my own, your daughter has enough of her own. If you add two enoughs together, the total will never spell poverty.
MUROMSKY.	No, of course not.
KRECHINSKY.	So, it is not wealth you are seeking?
MUROMSKY.	No. I am not seeking wealth.
KRECHINSKY.	Then what are you worried about? Or perhaps you have heard that my affairs are a bit run down?
MUROMSKY.	I must admit there has been talk of it.
KRECHINSKY.	But, tell me, whose affairs are not run down while living in Moscow? Take yourself. How much of a fortune have you made since you have been living here?
MUROMSKY.	Heaven help us! It's all been a dead loss.
KRECHINSKY.	There you are—a dead loss! We, landowners, are plagued by one evil, the evil of city life.
MUROMSKY.	It's a great truth you've just stated. City life is nothing but evil.
KRECHINSKY.	I'm leaving Moscow.
MUROMSKY.	You mean—back to the country?
KRECHINSKY.	Back to the country.
MUROMSKY.	You mean—you enjoy living in the country?
KRECHINSKY.	(*With emotion*) You, sir, don't know what irresistible means you possess to make anyone love the country! (*Takes Lidochka by the hand*) Your daughter! We love one another, sir, and we shall love living in the country. We shall live with you. Not a step from you. We shall labor together and share alike.
LIDOCHKA.	Papà, my dear papà!

KRECHINSKY.	Remember what I said a short while ago: the gray old man and his grandson? I meant you . . .
LIDOCHKA.	He meant you! (*They all surround Muromsky*)
MUROMSKY.	(*Retreats*) No, no . . . Not yet. Wait a bit . . . I never thought . . .
ATUYEVA.	Don't! Don't think! This is fate, the will of God!
MUROMSKY.	(*Looks at them, sighs*) Perhaps it is the will of God. Well, God bless you. Here is her hand. Only remember . . .
KRECHINSKY.	What, sir?
MUROMSKY.	Your promise about the gray-haired old man.
KRECHINSKY.	(*Leads Lidochka up to him*) Here is my guarantee! Do you believe me now?
MUROMSKY.	God grant it.
KRECHINSKY.	Anna Antonovna. (*Leads Lidochka up to Atuyeva*) You, too, give us your blessing.
ATUYEVA.	You see, he has not forgotten me. (*Embraces Lidochka and Krechinsky*) My children, be happy!
LIDOCHKA.	(*Kisses her*) Dear Auntie! Oh, how my heart is beating! . .
ATUYEVA.	This is as should be. It is beating with happiness.
MUROMSKY.	(*Strokes Lidochka's hair*) You are not going to cry now, my little soul?
LIDOCHKA.	No, papà, I am so happy!
KRECHINSKY.	Imagine, sir, just imagine the cattle farm you and I will establish! You'll see for yourself how businesslike I can be.
MUROMSKY.	Really?
KRECHINSKY.	Yes sir! I'll tell you (*talks as though he were disclosing a secret*) we'll breed nothing but a special strain of Poland China pigs recently developed in England.

SCENE XVI

Enter Nelkin. Stops just inside
the door, amazed.

MUROMSKY.   But the Poland China breed is . . . how shall I put it . . . they are very delicate pigs.

KRECHINSKY.   (*Kissing Lidochka's hand*) No, not exactly. Not delicate.

MUROMSKY.   God's truth—delicate.

NELKIN.   (*Walks in rapidly*) What's all this? Who's delicate?

KRECHINSKY.   (*Turns to face Nelkin*) Swine!

Curtain

ACT II

Krechinsky's Apartment. Morning.

SCENE I

A study luxuriously furnished, but in great disorder. Tables and bronze figures. On one side of the stage a bureau faces the audience. On the other, a table. Fyodor is tidying the room leisurely.

FYODOR.

(*Keeps sighing slowly and deeply*) The things that go on in this house . . . The devil's own doings! You'd never believe it. The place hasn't been heated for four days now. The rooms are cold as ice . . . What else can they be with nothing to heat them? (*Pause*) But when we lived in St. Petersburg—Heavenly Father!—the money that rolled in and out! And the gambling! . . He's been that way all his life—money burns in his hands like so much tinder. When he was still at the university he'd go off on binges often enough, but after he left, life became one mad whirlpool! Society, counts, princes, drunken sprees, cards! The golden youth crowd—they wouldn't make a move without him. The weaker sex—the same thing all over again. How many of them he's had—I can't even count that high. Whether it's the kind of taste they have, or some magic, they swarm around him like bees. No end to their letters, love notes, *bi-llet-doux*, personal calls. Those calls—oh, what a mess!

The women plead . . . and they love . . . and they hate and they are jealous. There was one woman, and what a woman she was! Rich and, let me tell you, as pretty as a doll. She'd kneel before him and stand that way by the hour, God is my witness. A rich woman like that, and on her knees kissing his hand like a slave. He had such power over her, poor soul . . . Money meant nothing to her. She'd have pawned her body for him three times over. But he—no, he would say, I don't want any woman's money, not that kind of money. Then he would clench his powerful fist and say: "I'm going to have money; I want to splurge!" And off he'd go! He'd cook up orgy after orgy . . . scares me even to think about it! . . He'd blow everything to the last kopek. And she—she wore herself to a shadow, poor thing. They say she died some-where abroad . . . Yes, we've seen everything and done everything, my friends, and nothing to show for it. And now, what is there to say? He had an estate in Simbirsk—gone as though it had never existed. He had race horses—sold them, for a song. And also the family silver, and even some of his own clothes. As if the earth had swallowed it all. As if the evil one took it. All his friends worth their salt, they've given him up, and instead only this fellow Raspluyev is hanging on to our coattails. But what good is he? If he walked around a tree, he'd never find his way home. (*Bell rings*) Speak of the devil! Barely sun-up, but in he comes for his meal, and to have me fix the playing cards for him as though he were somebody. "I can't do it myself," he says, "I play in such company." What kind of company? Last night he went off somewhere, grabbed two decks . . . the most carefully stacked decks . . . Maybe he did win some money, God grant . . . (*Another ring. Sighs*) I better let him in.

SCENE II

Raspluyev and Fyodor

RASPLUYEV. (*Untidily dressed, distraught, wearing a hat out of shape*) So, it's come to that? You don't want to let me in?

FYODOR. Begging your pardon, sir. I didn't hear you ring.

RASPLUYEV. (*Walks to the front of the stage and pauses, sighs*) Oh, what a life!

FYODOR. (*Aside*) He's not himself today.

RASPLUYEV. My God, oh my God, what does it all mean? Such goings on, my friends! My head (*points*) . . . would you believe it? Money . . . cards . . . destiny . . . happiness . . . a horrible, evil delirium! . . Oh, life! life! . . There was a time, there was a nice little fortune . . . They devoured it all, damn them, used it all up . . . Left me a beggar.

FYODOR. (*Walking up to Raspluyev*) Any luck, Ivan Antonich? Was there a game?

RASPLUYEV. (*Fixing him with a long stare*) Yes, there was a game. Take my word for it, there was a game! . . (*Sits down, moans*) My God, oh, my God!

FYODOR. What's eating you? Did you get into a mess?

RASPLUYEV. (*Fixes him with a long stare, spits on the floor*) That's what I got into! . . (*Pause*) What can one do? I admit. I did try to change the pack on the sly, and they did catch me red-handed . . . And then it started—biff bang, biff bang, biff bang! . . . So, he hit me! He hit me once, twice! Fine, I say, get your satisfaction and leave me alone. But no! Whoever heard of such a thing! He kept at it until he beat me senseless. I see, it's a bad business. His friends got all riled up—and they, too . . . (*Demonstrates*) I tried to give them the slip . . . But then, one of them, with the ungodliest mug (*shows an ungodliest mug*)—he wasn't even in the game—got up from the table, rolled up his sleeves. Leave him to me, he says, I'll give him a lesson in boxing! He raised a fist, the size of an elephant (*shows the size of the fist*) and pow! God pity me! "I'll make kindling out of him," he kept saying. (*Points at himself*) And so he did . . .

FYODOR.   (*In a moralizing tone*) Playing cards, Ivan Antonich, isn't the same as knitting socks. No, sir. They taught you a lesson.

RASPLUYEV.   That was no lesson! . . . No dog could take such a thrashing. No, that was no lesson. It was murder!

FYODOR.   Hm . . . murder? You slipped your hand in another man's pocket—why shouldn't he take a crack at you? Anybody would.

RASPLUYEV.   Strong as a bull—that's what he was! Wow! I've been in tight spots in my day, but let me tell you, I never expected a thrashing like this. Sometimes I had my innings, too, landed a good one in the snout—the snout, you know, is the first thing to aim for—but last night, no, that was something else again . . . (*Krechinsky in a dressing gown appears at the side door. Raspluyev does not notice him*) Last night, he must have had a system, that boxer. He didn't lash out at random, the dog, but rammed his big fist smack in my face. No, brother, you won't do it to me again. I've learned my lesson. I've sat in a corner for ten days at a stretch unable to work or swallow food—with a pair of shiners the like of which you never saw . . . (*Demonstrates*) I've learned my lesson thoroughly . . .

SCENE III

Krechinsky walks into the room, goes up to Raspluyev, examines him sternly. Motions to Fyodor to leave the room. Exit Fyodor.

KRECHINSKY. They broke you again?

RASPLUYEV. Broke me? Where did you get that idea?

KRECHINSKY. I can smell it. None of your tricks, you blockhead.

RASPLUYEV. Why am I a blockhead? Why do you keep raking me over the coals day after day? Good Lord, what a life! . .

KRECHINSKY. You're a windbag, that's what you are, a broken wheel that keeps churning water to no good purpose. (*Pause*) Do you earn the bread you eat? Are you worth your keep? Jackass! I am not feeding you out of charity! I do not subscribe to philanthropic societies. If you want to eat, you must bring in money. So, hand it over, damn you! Why do you keep staring at the floor? Start talking. Where were you last night?

RASPLUYEV. Yes . . . I was . . . What's that place . . . there . . . (*Points*)

KRECHINSKY. Did you bring any money?

RASPLUYEV. No money.

KRECHINSKY. Hand over the cash you took to start the game.

RASPLUYEV.	(*Spreading his arms*) Gone! It's all gone! . .
KRECHINSKY.	What do you mean gone?
RASPLUYEV.	Took it, all of it!
KRECHINSKY.	Blockhead! They took your money and gave you a beating on top of it. (*Angrily*) I should shake you by the scruff of your neck until your teeth rattle! (*Paces about the room in agitation*)
RASPLUYEV.	(*Whining*) Don't take the trouble, Mikhail Vasilich, I've hardly a tooth left. And I've already had my shaking. It will last me for a while. He's strong as a bull, let me tell you. I'll give him a boxing lesson, says he. (*To Krechinsky who keeps on pacing the room*) Permit me to ask, sir, what exactly is this boxing?
KRECHINSKY.	You of all people ought to know. (*Demonstrates*) This is what they call boxing. An English invention.
RASPLUYEV.	(*Imitates*) So, this is boxing! An English invention! Oh, God, my God! (*Shakes his head*) The English . . . a nation of culture, enlightened navigators . . .
KRECHINSKY.	I must get money! I must—no matter what! Money, and more money!
RASPLUYEV.	(*Indifferently*) Can't help you, Mikhail Vasilich, there's no money, and no way to get any. (*Sinks in thought. Suddenly, with heat*) Well! I never! The English! . . A civilized nation . . . Navigators of the seven seas . . .
KRECHINSKY.	(*Still pacing*) What are you mumbling about?
RASPLUYEV.	I was saying: the English, a nation of culture, aren't they?
KRECHINSKY.	You must be clean out of your mind.—I am talking to him about a serious matter, and he keeps jabbering about the devil knows what.— Listen carefully. There's only one thought in my head, one thought only: Money! Just

money! Go and get it, no matter where or how. My whole future, my life, everything, depends on a mere three thousand rubles. Go and bring it to me! Do you hear? Pawn your soul! No, forget about the soul . . . Steal the money, if you have to, only get it. Go to Bek, to Sprengel, to Starov, to all the moneylenders . . . Pay any interest they ask . . . Pay a hundred thousand rubles, only bring me that money. Don't come back empty-handed, or I'll wring your neck like a chicken! Bring that money! (*Pause*) Here's the whole story. I'm going to marry Muromsky's daughter. You know them. She's a good catch. It was all arranged last night. In ten days there'll be a wedding.

RASPLUYEV.   (*Stupefied*) Mikh . . . Mikh . . . Mikhail Vasilich! Is it really true?

KRECHINSKY.   A fortune—I have it all in my hands . . . Fifteen hundred serfs—worth a million and a half—and two hundred thousand cash. With that much cash I can win two million. And I shall, by God! It's a sure thing. I'll rake in the whole devilish amount, and then I'll settle down. Peace, a house of my own, a gullible wife, and a quiet, venerable old age. I'll give you two hundred thousand—enough to last you a lifetime, to give you independence, banquets, honors, influential friends, everything!

RASPLUYEV.   (*Bows, rubs his hands, laughs*) Two hundred thousand . . . banquets, ha, ha, ha . . . (*laughs*)

KRECHINSKY.   But first we need money. We have to hold out for another ten days. Without three thousand in cash right away, I'll be bankrupt by tomorrow. The men to whom I lost at cards will take out writs against me. They'll report me to the club, my name will be posted on the billboard

48

—that will finish me. Now do you understand?
(*Taking him by the collar*) Do you understand
how the lack of money is like a noose around
my neck, like a raging thirst! You've got to
bail me out!

RASPLUYEV. Mikhail Vasilich! My benefactor! Your words
make every nerve in my body tingle! I'm on my
way . . . (*Suddenly feeling pain*) Ouch! Ouch!
(*Collects himself*) My God! (*Exit*)

SCENE IV

Krechinsky (alone. Paces the room)

KRECHINSKY. He'll pull it off, I think. He's clever at this sort
of thing, he'll comb the whole city. Those
Judases know me . . . But what if he fails?
What then? God, how one needs money sometimes! (*Drums with his fingers*) There are times
in a man's life when he sees absolutely everything clearly . . . (*Thinks*) What if there is no
money? What if Raspluyev brings not a kopek?
What if that fat million slips through my
fingers for lack of a niggardly three thousand?
And at a time when everything is cooked,
baked, roasted, ready to pop into one's mouth
. . . It breaks my heart even to think of it . . .
(*Deep in thought*) Too bad I've been mixing
with such riff-raff lately. Nothing but wicked-
ness and trouble will come of it. Decent people
and those pompous noblemen have been giving
me a wide berth lately. Hm . . . they smelled a
rat. The only thing for me to do was to call it
quits—or pack up and leave. But then, as if on
purpose, along comes this blessed Muromsky
brood. A stupid waltz leads to a most contempt-

ibly banal flirtation. Matters come to a head quickly: yesterday—the consent; in ten days the wedding. I am making what is known as an excellent match. I'll have a house, status in the world, and a heap of friends and admirers . . . No, I can't complain! (*Gleefully*) And the card games to come! the gambling! With two hundred thousand I can win a mountain of gold. I can? I must! I'll simply have to fleece these fat sheep around me. But I won't live in the same house with that old fool. No, thank you! As for Lidochka, I'll have to take her firmly in hand, put her through some rigorous training, get her under my thumb so that there won't be a peep out of her—one thing I hate is whining women. But that won't be difficult, it seems. This Lidochka—the devil take her! . . she's a boiled turnip . . . some kind of a zero . . . I'll slip off to St. Petersburg. That's where the real gambling is! Here—nothing but small fry . . . trash . . .

SCENE V

Enter Fyodor

FYODOR. The merchant Shchebnev is here. Shall I ask him in?

KRECHINSKY. (*To himself*) This is what I have to face now—reality. (*To Fyodor*) You should have told him, you fool, that I was out.

FYODOR. No use, Mikhail Vasilich. You can't put off his kind. He'll sit like a log for eight hours in the front room, if he has to. He won't mind.

KRECHINSKY. All right. Let him in. (*Exit Fyodor*)

SCENE VI

Enter Shchebnev, dressed in the height of fashion. A huge gold chain, velvet, checkered waistcoat, loud, checkered trousers.

KRECHINSKY. (*Glibly*) Good morning, Timofey Tikhomirych.

SHCHEBNEV. Our respects, sir. In good health, I hope?

KRECHINSKY. I'm somewhat under the weather . . .

SHCHEBNEV. Perhaps a slight cold?

KRECHINSKY. That must be it.

SHCHEBNEV. There's a small balance due me after last night's game. May I have it?

KRECHINSKY. But didn't I tell you yesterday I'd bring it over myself?

SHCHEBNEV. So you did. Only, to tell the truth, we need the money. Do us the favor, let us have it, please.

KRECHINSKY. On my honor, I've no money right now. I'm expecting some any minute, and I'll deliver it to you without delay. (*Pause*) Well, what is going on at the club?

SHCHEBNEV. Nothing much, sir.

KRECHINSKY. Who joined the game after I left yesterday?

SHCHEBNEV. Oh, the usual crowd. Now, er . . . about the money, Mikhail Vasilich. Do us the favor.

KRECHINSKY. You're a strange one, Timofey Tikhomirych. Judge for yourself: how can I give you the money if I haven't got it? Simply haven't got it. What would you have me do—drum it out of the table with my bare hand?

SHCHEBNEV. So . . . as you wish . . . as you wish, sir. Only take no offense if we now go . . . well . . . to the club . . . and enter your name in the little book.

KRECHINSKY. (*Perturbed*) In the little book? You mean in the club book?

SHCHEBNEV. Yes, sir. It's the usual thing, you know . . .

KRECHINSKY. How can you say "the usual thing?" It means disgracing a man, killing him outright. The whole club will know about it today, and to-morrow—the whole town!

SHCHEBNEV. Of course, they will. The usual thing.

KRECHINSKY. (*Jumps out of the chair*) It may be usual for you, but most unusual for me. All my life I have paid my debts fully and on time. As a matter of fact, gracious sir, didn't I once wait three months for you, yes, precisely for you to pay up a debt? Do you remember?

SHCHEBNEV. So you did, Mikhail Vasilich. And we are for-ever grateful. But now, don't upset yourself, just do us a favor and give us what you owe. What can we do? Dire necessity.

KRECHINSKY. What dire necessity can you have? Allow me to ask, do you lose your right to put me down in the book tomorrow, or the day after? You don't lose that right, do you?

SHCHEBNEV. Yes, that's perfectly true.

KRECHINSKY. Then why insist on today?

SHCHEBNEV. The rules demand it, sir. No payment—down it goes in the little book.

KRECHINSKY. Really now, what's come over you? Am I re-fusing to pay? All I am asking is that you do me the honor of waiting two or three days. After all, I waited three months for you.

SHCHEBNEV. So you did. God's truth. But now, really, Mik-hail Vasilich, let's settle the account. Dire neces-sity, God knows.

KRECHINSKY. You won't give an inch, the devil take you! Or have you come here on purpose to play the fool? Why can't I knock it into your head that right now, at this moment, I have no money and therefore cannot give you any? Utterly impossible! (*Walks threateningly toward Shchebnev*) Is that clear?

SHCHEBNEV.   (*Rising*) Well, Mikhail Vasilich, you're all worked up about it, aren't you? The usual thing . . . (*Bows*) As you wish . . . (*After a pause he bows again and walks to the door*) Our best respects. Only, this evening, on my way to the club, I'll come around again. Please do us a favor, have it ready.

KRECHINSKY.   Ready, you say?

SHCHEBNEV.   The money, sir. Our best respects. (*Is about to leave*)

KRECHINSKY.   (*Seizes him by the hand*) Wait a minute! You can't do this! I sat down to play with you as with an honorable gentleman. No gentleman would keep choking another needlessly, or pin him against the wall without dire extremity. Then why, tell me, why are you choking the very life out of me? Why? What have I done to you? What have I ever done to you?

SHCHEBNEV.   Just as you wish, sir.

KRECHINSKY.   (*Meekly*) Please, listen to me. If you were without ready money as I am right now, then, of course, it would be a different story. But you have capital. You have money lying in that pawnshop of yours. You don't need it now. And I, I have never done you any harm! I even waited for you to pay me while you were collecting interest on my money.

SHCHEBNEV.   Have a heart, sir . . . How can you? . . . I swear . . .

KRECHINSKY.   That's neither here nor there. Why are you putting the squeeze on me so mercilessly? Why are you clubbing me to death? . . . Why?

SHCHEBNEV. (*After a pause*) Our best respects to you, Mikhail Vasilich. (*Heaves a sigh, bows and slips quietly through the door*)

SCENE VII

KRECHINSKY. (*Shouts after him*) Moneylender! (*Pause*) He'll do it! Sure as fate, he'll do it. He'll scribble my name in the book with that boorish scrawl of his, and the news will explode over Moscow like a clap of thunder. That will be the end. The end of everything! The wedding will fizzle out, and nothing will be left of that devilish million but a puff of smoke, a stench, a hangover and venom, yes, venom. (*Pause*) I don't mind saying, he'd better watch his step . . . (*With a hopeless gesture*) Stuff and nonsense! . . . I wonder if I won't have to pack up and sneak out of the city before they (*grabs himself by the collar*) . . . Become a tramp? . . . Oh, God . . . I'm in a jam! . . . (*Throws off his dressing gown*) Stifling hot! (*Paces in agitation*) Everything depends on Raspluyev! So, it's come to that . . . (*Sits down at the bureau, takes a sheet of paper and pencil and writes*) Let me figure out how much I need . . . I owe this one— fifteen hundred. That one (*points toward the door*) twelve hundred. As for this wolf—one thousand without fail. He raised such a howl, I'll have to shut his trap . . . that greedy trap. Throw in five or six hundred for the small fry. (*Adds up*) Where will I ever get all that money?

FYODOR. (*At the door*) The cabby's here, Mikhail Vasilich, asking for his money.

KRECHINSKY. In the neck! (*Exit Fyodor*) So, this is how I

stand. Three thousand rubles will get me nowhere . . . A drop in the bucket. And on top of it, the wedding! What will I use for the wedding? There'll be no end of expenses, unavoidable expenses. Every fool will be expecting gifts. Every swine will be waiting for a tip. Then come flowers, candy, basketfuls of silly trifles and all sorts of idiotic frippery . . . It all takes money . . . A lot of money! (*Thinks*) Money!

FYODOR. (*At the door*) The laundrywoman is here for her money, sir.

KRECHINSKY. In the neck!

FYODOR. The man who delivered firewood has been waiting for two hours.

KRECHINSKY. (*Raising his head*) Are you out of your mind? Don't you know your duty? Why do you bother me with all these trifles?

FYODOR. As you will, sir. I'm doing my best. Tried every trick . . .

KRECHINSKY. (*Half-rising*) Get out!

> (*Fyodor disappears behind the door. Clamoring voices are heard in the front room, gradually dying. Silence*)

SCENE VIII

> *Enter Raspluyev, heads straight toward the corner, discards his hat and slowly takes off his gloves.*

KRECHINSKY. (*Rises and looks at him searchingly, turns away, slowly folds his arms and faces the audience*) I knew it! (*His head sinks*) So! (*Pulls at his hair*) I knew it! . . . (*Slowly walks toward Raspluyev, his fists clenched. Raspluyev tries to retreat back stage. Krechinsky seizes him by the collar with both hands*)

RASPLUYEV. (*Timidly*) Mikhail Vasilich, allow me . . . they ask for security . . . secu . . .

KRECHINSKY. (*Rocking him back and forth violently*) But I ordered you . . . to get me . . . some money . . .

RASPLUYEV. Collateral . . . they want collateral . . . (*Gasping*) Mikh . . . Mikh . . .

KRECHINSKY. But I ordered you to steal, scoundrel! (*In a fit of fury*) I told you to cheat . . . rob! . . . (*Choking him*) Anything, but bring money! (*Raspluyev shouts. Krechinsky pushes him on to the settee, and walks off to a corner of the stage, his face unrecognizable*) So, he says there's no money! He's lying! There is money in every house . . . Of course, there is! The thing is to know where it's tucked away (*falls into a reverie, his fingers moving*) . . . yes, where it's tucked away . . . tucked away . . .

RASPLUYEV. (*Slowly gets on his feet, examines his jacket*) There you have it! (*Searches for buttons on the floor*) Two beatings in twenty-four hours! . . . Such a life is not worth living (*picks up a button*) . . . Such a life would make any dog leave home (*picks up another button*) . . . Take even the poodle, the most faithful dog there is . . . even a poodle would turn tail (*continues search*) . . . True, last night was different . . . an English thrashing . . . a lesson in boxing . . . But this—homemade stuff! . .

KRECHINSKY. (*Strikes his head with his fist. Moans*) Ah! Ah!

RASPLUYEV. (*Finds another button*) Ah, ah, ah! . . (*Picks it up*) How they do roll! The way he flew at me! What a temper!

KRECHINSKY. What shall I do? . . What shall I do? . .

RASPLUYEV. The first thing is, stop beating me. (*Con-

tinues his search for buttons, while Krechinsky sits down at the bureau. Silence) God, my God! Some people are born to happiness, to prosperity, to all the comforts, and their life, one might say, is one long banquet. But others are born to be drums, to be banged and buffeted from early dawn till late at night . . . One such man stands before you now. (*Faces the audience*) Well, had I been born skinny, delicate, puny, I never would have survived. God's truth, I never would. Take my word, I'd never have survived the boxing lesson I got yesterday. And that time last year—I'd never have survived that. And then the great drinking bout the year before—no earthly chance of surviving that . . . not a chance! But with all of this, I'm alive and in one piece. All I need is a square meal and a warm bed to snore in. (*Breaks off and watches Krechinsky search in a bureau drawer*) There's no money there, brother . . . (*Krechinsky opens another drawer*) nor there, either (*a third drawer*) nor there. Nowhere! No money, and yet he keeps on slapping people. What is he digging for? (*Krechinsky ransacks the drawer*) What does he expect to find in a drawer full of old rubbish? Money, that's what he's looking for, the old dear. But I know what's there—absolutely nothing! A lot of old letters from moneylenders, unpaid bills . . . (*Krechinsky produces a rather large pin*) Ah, he's found something— a piece of costume jewelry worth half a kopek!

KRECHINSKY. (*Suddenly exclaiming*) Ah! Eureka!

RASPLUYEV. Oho! (*Pressing himself against the wall*) He's raving . . . taking it too hard! (*Sighs*) Poverty is worse than a stepmother . . .

KRECHINSKY. (*Holding the pin*) Eureka! Eureka!

RASPLUYEV. God save me! He's mad! Raving mad!

KRECHINSKY. (*Suddenly thoughtful and speaking very slowly*) Eureka is a Greek word . . . it means . . . I have found it.

RASPLUYEV. Now he's talking Greek! . . My! . . (*Shakes his head*) This is the end of our earthly pilgrimage . . . Poor pigeon! . . . They'll take you, sweet friend, to the madhouse and keep you, God's servant, on a chain . . . This is the end of our earthly pilgrimage . . . (*Krechinsky deep in thought wags his index finger and mutters to himself, Raspluyev watching*) He's in a bad way . . . very bad . . . I better be on the lookout or he'll do me in . . . in his madness . . . my luck has been running that way . . . I better beat it while there's still time and I'm still in one piece. (*Takes his hat and tiptoes toward the door*) Oh, my sainted aunt! My sainted aunt! (*Exit Raspluyev*)

KRECHINSKY. Does it all really add up? (*Rubs his forehead*) Isn't there a mistake somewhere? (*Lost in thought again*)

RASPLUYEV. (*Reappearing at the door, with Fyodor*) Take a good look at him! The way he's carrying on!

KRECHINSKY. First this! Then this! Then this! (*Leaps*) Bravo! Hurrah! I have it, by God, I have it!

RASPLUYEV. (*Hiding behind the door*) Great doings! Off his nut, I'm telling you. Rocky to the very foundation! . . .

FYODOR. (*Approaches timidly and in embarrassment*) Mikhail Vasilich, dear sir, what's wrong? Have a glass of water. What ails you? Should I give you some smelling salts? Don't take it so hard, little father. We've been in worse fixes . . . and we'll get out of this one . . . I'll carry you away on my shoulders, just say the word.

KRECHINSKY. (*Listens attentively, speaks kindly*) Don't worry, Fyodor, I'm all right . . . (*Shouts*) Hey, Raspluyev! (*Raspluyev shudders from head to foot*) Go this very minute to that swanky flower shop, you know the one, and buy a bouquet of white camellias. The best they have, it's got to be white camellias. The best! Go and bring them this very minute.

RASPLUYEV. (*Pointing at Krechinsky, speaks tearfully to Fyodor*) What did I tell you? Not a broken coin in the house, and he blows fifty rubles on white camellias! (*Paces back and forth*) Oh, brother, my brother, what are we going to do? What are we, Fyodor, two poor orphans, going to do now?

KRECHINSKY. (*Stops pacing*) What? You're still here? Perhaps your ears are plugged up. I'll clean them for you. Didn't you hear me? (*Advances threateningly*) I ordered flowers!

RASPLUYEV. (*Retreating to the wall*) Mikh . . . Mikhail Vasilich, have mercy! What am I going to use for money? There isn't even a kopek in the house. Have mercy, be reasonable. How can I buy you camellias?

FYODOR. Get going, Ivan Antonich, get going. You heard the master order flowers. Get going.

RASPLUYEV. But what will I use for money? Where's the money? I haven't any.

KRECHINSKY. (*Takes his watch and chain off the table*) Here's the money. Hock it! I want the camellias here within half an hour. Get going! (*Exit Raspluyev*)

SCENE IX

KRECHINSKY.   And now . . . yes, now I must get a note ready for Lidochka. Time is precious . . . Down to business! (*Sits down at the bureau, starts writing*)

FYODOR.   (*Aside, looking sideways at Krechinsky*) Raspluyev was talking through his hat. The master is not mad. He's sitting there like an eagle. (*Exit*)

SCENE X

KRECHINSKY.   (*Writes, pausing from time to time*) No good! (*Tears the paper, writes again*) Started on the wrong foot again! (*Tears up the paper, writes again*) What the devil! The letter must be so written—that it would make a dead woman throb with passion! Passion arouses passion. Oh, passion! passion! where are you? (*Smiles scornfully*) My passion, my love . . . I'm searching for sparks in a fire gone dead . . . (*Snickers*) But I must, I really must! (*Writes, reads over, crosses out, writes again*) What a job: like sweating blood! . . . (*Wipes his face and reads the letter quickly*) Hm . . . hm . . . mm . . . my gentle angel . . . sweet family haven . . . hm . . . hm . . . hm . . . tender constellation . . . the devil knows what rot! Sheer gibberish . . . bird's milk and horse feathers . . . and so on . . . (*Seals the letter and writes the address*) But what I'm after is this: my gentle angel, please send me one of your sparkling wings—your pin with the diamond solitaire reflecting the brilliance of your heavenly abode. We must fit out a magic ship to sail under the four winds: the wind of spades, of hearts, of clubs, and of diamonds . . . over the troubled seas of life. I shall be at the helm. Raspluyev will rig the sails . . . and you will be our ballast! Still no sign of Raspluyev . . . what the . . .

SCENE XI

Enter Raspluyev

KRECHINSKY. There you are! At last!

RASPLUYEV. (*Carefully carrying a bouquet; points at it as he addresses the audience*) Twenty-five rubles for this broom. Pah!

KRECHINSKY. Come here. Let me see. (*Inspects*) Handsome. It'll do. The change?

RASPLUYEV. (*Disappointed*) The change? Fifty rubles. (*Hands over the money*)

KRECHINSKY. Now button your lip and listen to me. It's a tricky business. Here is a letter for my fiancée, Lidya Petrovna Muromskaya, just around the corner on the boulevard. You know? . . .

RASPLUYEV. (*Coming to life*) I know, Mikhail Vasilich, I know. Just as you turn the corner, there's a huge white house with a driveway.

KRECHINSKY. That's it. What time is it? About one?

RASPLUYEV. (*Skipping up to the clock*) A quarter to.

KRECHINSKY. Right. The old man won't be home. About this time he drives around the town with those pitiful nags of his. Go straight to the house and hand the bouquet to Lidya Petrovna. Wish her a good morning for me, you know how . . . with a flourish, a bit of swank, ingratiate yourself . . . understand? And tidy yourself up. Put my jacket on . . . Hey, Fyodor! (*Enter Fyodor*) Give him my jacket. If the old man should be at home, give her the bouquet but keep the note out of sight. In it, among other things, I'm asking her to send me the diamond solitaire which I had made over into a pin . . . remember?

RASPLUYEV.   (*Puts on the jacket with Fyodor's help*) I know, I remember. Twenty carats. Worth thirty thousand.

KRECHINSKY.   I'm telling her that I had an argument with Prince Belsky about the pin last night and that I placed a big bet on it.

RASPLUYEV.   (*Makes a noise expressing understanding and admiration*)

KRECHINSKY.   Get the pin and bring it here without fail. (*Threatens him*) About the wager, you can throw in a few lies of your own.

RASPLUYEV.   I'll lie, Mikhail Vasilich. Always happy to oblige with a lie.

KRECHINSKY.   On the other hand, you'd better not lie. You always overdo it. Run along, but once you've got the pin, fly! Watch out for the old man. The rest will go like clockwork. Understand?

RASPLUYEV.   (*In a low voice*) I understand, Mikhail Vasilich. (*Raises his brows and index finger meaningfully*) I understand! I'm off!

SCENE XII

KRECHINSKY.   (*Alone*) He says he understands . . . The fool doesn't understand anything. He thinks I want to steal the solitaire. He thinks I'm a thief. Oh, no, brother, we still value our reputation. We still have resources left in this pocket (*points at his head*). Now to work. Fyodor! Hey, Fyodor! (*Fyodor comes rushing in through the door*) Where were you? Taking a nap?

FYODOR. No, sir, I only have two legs.

KRECHINSKY. If two legs aren't enough, get a third! . . Here is money. The first thing, get the rooms heated. Only take it easy. Otherwise you'll heat them hot as hell for sheer joy. It's too early for that. Next, I'm having six persons for tea this evening: my fiancée and her relatives, that Nelkin fellow, and perhaps one or two others. Everything must be first rate.

FYODOR. Yes, sir. Will you serve dessert?

KRECHINSKY. Everything must be first rate. Light the candles, but not in the chandelier. Tidy up the rooms. Fumigate them with sweet herbs. Hang decorations all over the place. The reception is at seven.

FYODOR. What about livery?

KRECHINSKY. No livery. The servants will wear tails and white ties and waistcoats. And close the drapes, yes, close the drapes. Remember, it isn't a merchant's daughter being married. It is a gentleman giving a reception.

FYODOR. Yes, sir. (*Exit hurriedly*)

SCENE XIII

KRECHINSKY. And now I must find two pieces of paper as alike as two drops of water. Let's not rush. (*Rummages in the bureau*) There! The very thing! Dunning letters. Couldn't be better. (*Places one on top of the other and cuts them in half with scissors*) Splendid! (*Sings an air from "Der Freischutz"*)

"In this vale of pain and grief
Only wine can bring relief."

You're all wrong, Freeshooter. The song should go like this:

"In this vale of pain and grief
Only brains can bring relief
From ill-luck and sorrow. (*Repeat*)
Brains will keep you fit and gay.
If you're penniless today,
Brains will make you rich tomorrow."

(*Ends the song with an incredible roulade*) And the moment you hit the word "rich" in the song, you can roll your roulades any old way you please. However wildly off-key you are—fine! Anything goes! Yes, brains are everything! Everywhere—brains! In society—brains. In love—brains. In gambling—brains. In theft—brains! Yes, yes, here it is—a philosophy has popped up. When I counted on Raspluyev, there wasn't any philosophy. Yes, even this daughter of Socrates seems to prefer good soil to bad . . . But . . . I hope Raspluyev won't make a mess of things: he's been gone for half an hour, if not more. And now, at this moment, at this great moment, we are crossing the Rubicon, reaching the other side, or . . . or sinking in a bottomless whirlpool. Yes, this is it! The decisive moment! (*Noises. Raspluyev comes running in in his overcoat, out of breath. Krechinsky rushes to meet him*)

SCENE XIV

*Following, Fyodor helps
Raspluyev take off his overcoat.*

KRECHINSKY.   Well, Raspluyev, victory? Victory?

RASPLUYEV.   Victory, Mikhail Vasilich, victory! Here it is, on the hook! She swallowed the bait. (*Holds the pin high in the air, hands it to Krechinsky*)

KRECHINSKY.   (*Gaily*) Bravo, Raspluyev, the Rubicon is crossed!

RASPLUYEV.   (*Skipping with glee*) Crossed!

KRECHINSKY.   The Rubicon.

RASPLUYEV.   The Rubicon!

KRECHINSKY.   Idiot!

RASPLUYEV.   Idi . . . no, oh no, Mikhail Vasilich, not an idiot. Remarkable—the way I pulled it off. I arrive, I come in and ask: Is the master at home? No, they say, he is not at home. Is the young lady at home, says I. Yes, they say, the young lady is at home. Where is the young lady, says I. In her room, they say. Announce me, says I. Yes . . .

KRECHINSKY.   Yes. Sheer genius on your part . . . (*Withdraws to the bureau. Raspluyev joins Fyodor and goes on with the story, gesticulating. Krechinsky compares the two pins*) Like two drops of water. (*Wraps each separately in the paper he had prepared*) Foolproof! (*Places them in his wallet and turns to Raspluyev*) And now—on the run!

RASPLUYEV.   Run?! Well, I'm ready to run.

KRECHINSKY.   Grab everything you can. Step lively! (*To Fyodor*) Let's get dressed.

RASPLUYEV.   (*Running about the room*) Fyodor! Come, brother, grab everything you can. Hurry! (*Picks

up whatever comes to hand, runs past Kre-
chinsky, trips, falls)

KRECHINSKY. (*Dressing*) Hurry, brother, hurry! Bring my traveling case. (*Raspluyev runs into the next room, brings the traveling case*) Hold everything! It's no use, brother. (*Raspluyev stops as though petrified*) Suppose they send mounted police after us, they'll catch us in no time.

RASPLUYEV. Mounted police? Yes, they'll overtake us in no time.

KRECHINSKY. They'll collar us and off we go to Siberia.

RASPLUYEV. Yes, if they collar us, off we go to Siberia.

KRECHINSKY. Then what shall we do with the pin?

RASPLUYEV. Yes, what shall we do with the pin?

KRECHINSKY. Fyodor!

RASPLUYEV. Fyodor!

KRECHINSKY. Bring my overcoat.

RASPLUYEV. Bring both our overcoats.

KRECHINSKY. (*Quickly puts on his overcoat*) No, my friend, no overcoat for you. By all rights you should be wearing a prisoner's stripes. (*Pauses at the door*) Fyodor, don't let him out of here. Not for a second. Hear me? (*Exit*)

FYODOR. Yes, master. (*Posts himself at the door and bolts it under Raspluyev's nose*)

SCENE XV

RASPLUYEV. (*Standing as though petrified*) Wait! What are you doing! Mikhail Vasilich! . . . (*At the top of his voice*) Mikhail Vasilich! . . Where is he going? Let me go, Fyodor. Let go of me, let go of me, I tell you! What's got into you? (*Tries to push Fyodor away from the door*) What's got into you?

FYODOR. (*Holds him at bay with one hand*) Be so good as to stay, sir. You heard the master.

RASPLUYEV. (*Completely baffled*) What? But this . . . this is slaughter! . . . treachery! . . . (*Screams*) Treachery! (*Returns to the door and tries to push Fyodor aside*) Let me out, brigand, let me out, I tell you! (*Fyodor turns the key in the lock*) Oh, saints in heaven! Murder! Help! Murder! He-e-e-elp! (*Suddenly quiets down*) Sh . . . sh . . . What am I doing? Digging my own grave? They'll swoop down and grab me . . . Let me go, Fyodor, let me go, dear brother . . . After all, it makes no difference to you . . . What will you get out of destroying my sinful soul? The police will be here any minute, on the trail. As soon as the old man comes home, they'll pick up my trail. Who was here? they will say. Why, Raspluyev was here, Ivan Antonich! Hand the scoundrel over to us, they'll say . . . The old man is rich, important, so they'll grab me like this . . . (*takes himself by the collar*) in tow . . . then to the governor-general, then to the court, and then I get my marching orders to Siberia! (*Sits down on the traveling case and weeps*) Fyodor, Fyodor, will it give you any pleasure or profit to see me flogged at the whipping post?

FYODOR. For pity's sake! . . . How can they flog a nobleman? Nonsense!

RASPLUYEV. What kind of a nobleman am I? Rot and a contemptible lie! My title was conferred on me by the king of spades, and that's all there is to it. Please, Fyodor, brother! Let me go. For the love of Christ! I have a little nest . . . with fledglings . . . waiting for me to bring food . . .

FYODOR.	What are you talking about? What kind of a nest?
RASPLUYEV.	A regular family nest, with little tots. The tiny fledglings will die of cold and hunger without me. They'll be thrown out on the street like a litter of mangy pups. Children, Fyodor, our flesh and blood! . . .
FYODOR.	Calm down, Ivan Antonich, stop worrying. Where could the master have gone?
RASPLUYEV.	Where? To the four winds.
FYODOR.	Is he the sort who runs to save his skin? He'll land on his feet. He's attending to some business, not running away.
RASPLUYEV.	No, he's gone. I swear he's gone. Why should he worry about us? This stone, they say, is worth forty thousand, that's the kind of a stone it is! But who am I to complain? The very second I felt the damned thing in my pocket and sniffed the fresh air, it began to devil me. But what held me back was this thought: where could I go with it? I? Where? He'd swoop down on me like a hawk on a chicken! Now he has nothing to worry about. All roads are open to him. So off he rides without a care in the world.
FYODOR.	What has he to gain by running away, especially with stolen goods. A fool would run, not he.
RASPLUYEV.	You mean to say, he'll be sporting about town with a stolen diamond?
FYODOR.	Who said stolen?
RASPLUYEV.	We tricked the girl out of it. What else can he do with it? Skip town and that's all there is to it.
FYODOR.	Well . . . he's gone to pawn it.
RASPLUYEV.	Pawn it? But it has to be returned tonight, or

else the police will return it . . . and send us off to Siberia. But who wants to go to Siberia? No, brother, he's gone, simply gone. And you and I must go, too.

FYODOR.   What do I have to do with it? I belong here.

RASPLUYEV.   You'll rot in prison.

FYODOR.   What for? I know nothing. All I do is sweep rooms, shine shoes. I know nothing and wish to know nothing. That will be my line. But, as you say, it does look somewhat shady. Perhaps the master has gone away somewhere, who knows?

RASPLUYEV.   Gone away? . . . but that means he has run away . . . (*Clutches his head and bustles about the room; whines, moans, stops, and pulls himself together*) Look, Fyodor, if they ask you, remember! You saw with your own eyes that I gave him the pin.

FYODOR.   What?

RASPLUYEV.   (*Shouting*) I say you saw with your own eyes, on this very spot, how I handed over the pin to that brigand, your master.

FYODOR.   Please, Ivan Antonich. Don't drag me into this. It's not my place to meddle in such things. I shine shoes, sweep the rooms. I know nothing about your affairs.

RASPLUYEV.   (*In horror*) Judas! What do you mean you know nothing? You saw me give it to him right here, under your very nose! . . .

FYODOR.   Have mercy . . . How should I know what you gave him? You said nothing to me about what you gave him.

RASPLUYEV.   Brute! Brute! (*Beats his head against the wall*) You've done me in! . . . (*Moans*) The devil's own gang! I see it all now! You're holding an axe over my head! . . But no, I won't let you! . .

	(*In desperation*) Let me go, I tell you, let me go, soulless wretch! . . Let me go! (*Leaps on Fyodor. They struggle in silence, panting for breath. Fyodor finally pins him down*)
FYODOR.	No use, brother, no use, I'm telling you, Ivan Antonich. Stop wriggling . . . Stop, I'm telling you. (*Clutches at his throat*)
RASPLUYEV.	(*Groans and moans*) Let go of me . . . You're choking me . . . I'm dying . . . Have mercy . . .
FYODOR.	(*His hands still on Raspluyev's throat*) Orders are orders. Keep still.
RASPLUYEV.	(*Breaks away, walks to the foreground, straightens out his clothes*) Whew! . . Ah, ah, ah . . . (*Addresses the audience*) Would you believe it, this damned fool would be only too happy to choke me to death . . . (*Pause*) My third drubbing in two days! By God, three of them! (*Folds his arms*) Fate! (*Louder*) Fate! Why do you persecute me? Why do you pers . . . (*Catches sight of Fyodor*) Look at this devilish mug! Stands at the door like a wooden image. No feelings . . . (*Fyodor looks at him with indifference. Raspluyev looks around*) But time is flying. Time is flying! They may already be on their way here! And I am trapped and must wait in silence for the blow . . . prison . . . to wait for retribution in silence! I must wait and say nothing, do nothing . . . God, my God, how my heart sinks . . . aches . . . the pain is right here, the suffocation . . . My babies, naked and cold . . . Will I ever see you again? My little Vanya . . . (*Weeps. Bell rings*) Ah! They've come! The police! The police! (*Runs back and forth about the room. Another ring. Fyodor leaves to open the door*) They've come! . . . They're here! . . . (*Throws himself in despair on the suitcase*)

SCENE XVI

*Krechinsky enters rapidly, followed by Fyodor
who tells him something in a low voice.*

KRECHINSKY. (*In high spirits*) Ha,ha,ha! Well done, Fyodor,
well done! (*To Raspluyev*) I hear, brother,
you've had a bit of a tussle while I was gone.
Excellent! It helps to pass away the time. Your
only trouble, Ivan Antonich, is that you are in
too much of a hurry. Everything in its own time.
That's the law of nature! The police will come,
Siberia will come. Don't worry, everything will
come in its own good time. Only don't rush
things. (*Goes to the bureau, unwraps a package*)
In the meantime, here is something to keep
you busy. (*Hands him a substantial pack of
bills*) Count this money, little brother, break it
up into small packets. There are debts to pay.
It's our duty, our sacred duty. As for the pin
(*places it on the table*), it must be returned
tonight. This is the way honest people do business. And you thought! . . .

RASPLUYEV. (*Utterly shaken, staggers to the table*) I simply
don't see a thing. Just a blur of spots and stripes
. . . (*Rubs his forehead*) I see money! Money!
And there . . . there . . . the pin! Yes, the pin!
(*Starts counting the money*) One hundred . . .
two hundred . . . four hundred . . . nine hundred . . . fourteen . . . phew! (*Begins the count
all over. To the audience*) Let me tell you something, ladies and gentlemen. Right here in Moscow (*sighs*) I once watched the great magician
and professor of Egyptian mysteries, the great
Bosko! He could pour wine out of his hat
(*whimpers*), red wine and white wine; he could

load pistols with canaries; he could pick bunches of roses out of his fist and present them to the ladies in the audience . . . But—I pledge you my soul and all its many sins—that he never could have brought off a trick like this! Ladies and gentlemen, compared with Krechinsky, Professor Bosko was but a babe-in-arms, a puppy!

KRECHINSKY. (*Writing at the table*) Quit your babbling! Count it! Forever wagging your tongue. This fellow has some kind of a sentimental streak. One minute you'd take him for a tree stump, and the next he's as soft as a jellyfish.

RASPLUYEV. (*In rapture*) God in Heaven! What blessed oil is it that anointeth my heart? What aroma is it that stealeth upon me from all sides? I can smell jasmine in the air . . . And altogether I'm probably blabbing such tommyrot that I shall later be ashamed of myself.

KRECHINSKY. (*Laughs*) You said it.

RASPLUYEV. Go ahead, laugh! Why shouldn't you laugh? You were born to laugh. Why shouldn't you? For you—a twist, a maneuver, and you're on top. But just you step into my shoes, and you'll change your tune. Ask Fyodor! Without you I was a lost man . . . a kind of cloudiness came over me. I sat there (*points at the suitcase*) and howled like a wolf.

KRECHINSKY. Cut it out! I'm waiting. How much longer will it take you?

RASPLUYEV. Give a man a chance to rejoice, Mikhail Vasilich. (*Sorts out the money*) Here they are, the little darlings . . . My little doves . . . sweet larks! How is this for a little bunch of daisies and buttercups? And another bunch, and a third . . . sweet lilies of the fields . . . and yet another

bunch . . . and a third, and a fourth! . .
(*Laughs, giggles*) Oh, God in heaven, what
wouldn't I do for a pile like this? (*Sits down
to count. Silence*)

KRECHINSKY.   (*Puts on hat and coat, walks up to Raspluyev*)
Well, child, ready?

RASPLUYEV.   (*Hastily*) This minute . . . just one minute.

KRECHINSKY.   (*Takes one pack of bills*) This I'll deliver myself. And these—you take care of. Also, get my
watch back. Here is a list of people to repay.
Make sure, pay every last one of them.

RASPLUYEV.   (*Wraps the money carefully in a piece of paper*)
Tell me, Mikhail Vasilich, how come? This
money is from Bek the moneylender, isn't it?

KRECHINSKY.   Yes, from him.

RASPLUYEV.   Then how come the pin . . . wait (*examines the
pin*). Yes, it's the same treasure of my heart . . .
the very same pin Lidya Petrovna gave me . . .
Ah?

KRECHINSKY.   Of course, and tonight we return it. (*Takes the
pin from Raspluyev and locks it up in the
bureau*)

RASPLUYEV.   But why "of course?" The devil knows why "of
course?" How did you do it—get the money and
keep the pin?

KRECHINSKY.   You're a hound, Raspluyev, but you have no
scent, a wretched hound without scent . . .
(*both walk toward the door*)

Curtain

ACT III

Krechinsky's apartment, cleaned up and brightly lit. Evening of the same day.

SCENE I

Fyodor, in tails, white tie, white vest, and white gloves, fusses with the lamps and dusts the furniture. Enter Raspluyev, wearing tails and white gloves, sporting a permanent wave.

RASPLUYEV. (*Roars with laughter*) It's too much for me! (*Laughter*) I could die laughing. (*Hangs up his hat*) When I think of that villainous face, the way he sits there, the anti-Christ, with that piece of glass . . . guarding it, the Judas, under seven locks . . . a piece of cheap crystal framed in worthless brass! When I think of it . . . (*laughter*) I could die laughing. (*Pulls himself together*) I bet he keeps rubbing his hands. He gave six thousand rubles, what a pile! And thinks all the time: Krechinsky will go broke and the diamond solitaire is mine! Eh, Fyodor? Our Mikhail Vasilich is a second Napoleon, eh? Hand me a pencil. (*Fyodor obliges*) Wait, I'll write it down. What was it he said? Eureka or Eudrika?

FYODOR. I think it was Eureka.

RASPLUYEV. So be it—Eureka. I'll name my first bloodhound Eureka. Come here, Eureka, come here, little dog. Sounds pretty good. Remember, Fyodor, how he suddenly shouted Eureka, I found it? By God, he did find it.

FYODOR. There . . . you see? And you were ready to pack him off to a lunatic asylum.

RASPLUYEV. What can I say, brother, I slipped. But, do you know how he pulled it off?

FYODOR. How should I know? To tell the truth, I've never been a fool, but this thing is too deep for me. Whichever way I look at it, my brain simply freezes.

RASPLUYEV. (*With glee*) But I, I'll spell it out for you, brother. I'll spell it out! Only mind you—the thing's top secret!

FYODOR. For God's sake!

RASPLUYEV. Look, it's this way . . . (*Straightens his tails, gestures*) He started turning it over in his mind, turning it over, figuring it out this way and that way. Well, Raspluyev, says he, bail me out of this mess. At your service, Mikhail Vasilich, I say, I'm ready for anything. Here's what, says he, pawn your soul but get me that diamond solitaire. The same one, says he, I had made into a pin last fall, the same one I had modeled after that trinket in my bureau. This set me thinking.

FYODOR. Set you thinking?

RASPLUYEV. Yes, me. It's a tricky business, I say, tricky. But off I go, and in fifteen minutes back I fly like a hawk with its prey. Here! I say, here's the little dove. The way I figure it, he takes it, and he takes the model . . . get me? . . . The model from which the pin was copied, and slips them both in his wallet.

FYODOR. In his wallet . . .

RASPLUYEV.   Yes, his wallet. Oh, what a crook! Held on to the trinket . . . See? And it turned the trick! He takes the solitaire and the trinket, and goes straight to Bek the moneylender. Out with your money, Judas, says he, out with the money! —Money? What money? I've got no money.— But you've got it for a pledge? —For a pledge I've got it. And how much, for instance, says he, will you, Judas, give me for this little trinket? That shook him. He drooled, his eyes burned, and he trembled like in a fever. He tested it this way and that way, under the glass, on the scales, and he turned it, and he tasted it . . . He knows it's a diamond of the first water. Four thousand—Four thousand?! Son of a dog, it's worth ten. You must think I'm a sucker? Give it back—the deal is off! But Judas was all heated up, couldn't let the pin out of his hands. But Mikhail Vasilich snatched it from him and put it back in his wallet. Give me seven thousand! (*In falsetto*) I can't! I can't! Five!— I want seven— All right, six!—No!— Very well, good-bye! Remember me in your prayers. I'll get eight elsewhere. The brute trembles from head to foot . . . howls like a wolf . . . the beast:—Don't go, I'll take it.—It's a deal?—A deal!—In that case, fetch me some sealing wax and a box.—Why a box?—Plain as day. We'll tuck the diamond away in the box with our own hands, and then I'll seal it myself. It'll be safe that way. But this treasure is not for you, Judas! Get it? (*An exclamation of admiration*)

FYODOR   (*Nods*) Yes, yes!

RASPLUYEV.   (*Continues*) He ran for the box like a homing pigeon. And drag out the money, says Mikhail Vasilich. So, he drags out the money. Now, says the master, look at it, and he takes the pin out of his wallet—not the real diamond, but the model, you understand, the model . . . Flashes it under his nose . . . an Eldorado . . . a Mona Lisa . . . how's that?

FYODOR.   God in Heaven!

RASPLUYEV.   (*Worked up*) And his eyes are bloodshot—blinded—with greed . . . One, two . . . plunk into the box! Sealed it. Bek hands over the money, and keeps the box. Mikhail Vasilich comes straight here, shoots the money at me across the table . . . a pile this high! Count it, says he, and remember Mikhail Vasilich Krechinsky!

FYODOR.   (*Arms folded*) Oh, God in heaven! (*Both stand in worshipful silence*)

RASPLUYEV.   (*On top of the world*) A Napoleon, I tell you, a Napoleon! A great hero, a sorcerer and magician! He drew circles around him! Circles! He duped him, duped the man for all eternity! Did I say "man?" No! He duped a moneylender and thereby erected a great monument to himself!

FYODOR.   A clean job! My God, there's a clean job!

RASPLUYEV.   And how clean! A miracle! The money is here and the diamond is here. And tonight we shall return it with gratitude . . . (*With enthusiasm*) A piece of glass lies under seven seals and seven locks . . . Judas crouching over it with his unholy body. Not a trace, not a single trace! He'll settle his debts at the club, blow a fortune on the wedding, lay his hands on a million rubles and start raking in more . . . until he has piled up a mountain of gold . . . And he'll become a gentleman great and illustrious! And he won't forget us. Say, Fyodor, he won't forget us?

FYODOR.   It'll be fine if he doesn't.

RASPLUYEV.	He promised me two hundred thousand.
FYODOR.	It's good he promised. As the saying goes, the master promised me a sheepskin coat, and the promise keeps me warm.
RASPLUYEV.	Wha-a-at? Where did you dig up such a saying? He promised, of course, he promised. (*Bell*) It must be Mikhail Vasilich. And so it is. (*Raising his hands worshipfully*) Oh, great hero, sorcerer and magician! (*Goes respectfully to meet him*)

SCENE II

KRECHINSKY.	(*Enters, discards hat*) What a day! Eh? Get me a chair, Fyodor. I am tired. Tired for the first time in my life; must be getting old . . . Is everything in order here? (*Sits down. Fyodor and Raspluyev remain standing*)
FYODOR.	Everything in order, Mikhail Vasilich, according to instructions. Everything in order.
KRECHINSKY.	(*Inspects the room*) So I see. Very good. Put another candlestick there. Yes, quite an imposing place. No bridegroom would be ashamed of it. (*To Raspluyev, sternly*) Did you take care of everything?
RASPLUYEV.	Everything, Mikhail Vasilich, everything as you ordered, everything to a T. Do you want the receipts?
KRECHINSKY.	By all means. Your word is not enough. (*Scans the receipts*) Hmm . . . Good. Fyodor! Here, lock them in the bureau.
RASPLUYEV.	Your watch, Mikhail Vasilich, and the chain. That takes care of everything. (*Hands him the watch and chain*) I hope you noticed how I've attended to everything.

KRECHINSKY. Good. Phew! Am I tired. (*Attaches the chain to the watch*) Had an excellent meal at the club. I haven't had such an appetite for a long time. That fool Nelkin was there . . . Kept staring at me like an owl. Go ahead, old chap, keep staring. Your girl's been stolen right from under your nose. No use eyeing me now. I'm tough, my friend. I can bend horseshoes . . .

RASPLUYEV. I had a good meal, too, after I did all the errands.

KRECHINSKY. So, you didn't forget?

RASPLUYEV. For Heaven's sake, how could I? I strode in and sat down smack in the middle of the settee, chin in hand. Bring me a bowl of fish soup, say I, two fish pies, and a suckling pig—the whole of it! I couldn't believe myself: was it me or someone else? They brought the fish soup—none like it in the whole world: drops of amber chasing each other all over the bowl. I had just put the first spoonful in my mouth, when I remembered Bek sitting there like a fool . . . and I chuckled . . . the soup splurted all over me . . . even spotted my vest . . . damn it all.

KRECHINSKY. All right, all right. Listen. When the guests arrive, keep the old man busy, jabber away about anything. I'll stay with the women and fix it so there'll be a wedding within two days. But you'd better go easy with your fibs. Don't lay it on too thick.

RASPLUYEV. (*Offended*) Why would I put it on too thick? Why? I do all the work, and never a word of approval from you.

KRECHINSKY. To the devil with you and your approval! . . . You're a blockhead, born and bred. (*Thinking*) Let me see . . . are you dressed properly?

RASPLUYEV.   On my way from the restaurant, Mikhail Vasilich, I dropped in at the French hairdressers and had my hair done *à la mouzhik*. And then, kindly observe, I bought a pair of white gloves . . . white as white can be.

KRECHINSKY.   That wasn't at all necessary.

RASPLUYEV.   Have a heart! White gloves are a must! And then I got all decked out in your tails . . . look me over.

KRECHINSKY.   (*Bursts out laughing*) Handsome is the word! Just think of it. A real personage. (*Turns him around*)

RASPLUYEV.   Of course, Mikhail Vasilich, why shouldn't I be a personage? Money does everything. Without money, you wear your clothes threadbare, and run errands for others. But with money, I'd send others on errands, and I'd show them my displeasure.

KRECHINSKY.   All right, all right, enough! And now, step lively. Fyodor! (*Fyodor comes running in*) I want everything to perfection, dignified. No commotion from the servants. Make sure their hands are washed and their noses are wiped. Two waiters in the front room. Another candlestick here. The green table there. (*Looks at his watch*) They'll be coming any moment. All's well that ends well. Hold it! Fyodor! Over there, in the hallway, I saw a portrait . . . some old general with a mug like this (*grimace*). Dust it off, bring it in and hang it over my bureau. I need an ancestor . . . (*Servants place the candlestick, the table, the portrait. Bell*) Here they are! I'll show them in. You, Raspluyev, sit here on the sofa, like a big shot. Take the newspaper . . . the newspaper, you fool! Put on airs! Oh, what a blockhead! . . . (*Exit*)

RASPLUYEV.   (*To the audience*) You see, picking on me again. Only a minute ago he said handsome, handsome! Don't you forget, brother, you promised me two hundred thousand. You did.

SCENE III

Muromsky, Atuyeva, Lidochka, Krechinsky, and Raspluyev. Bows and handshaking.

MUROMSKY.   (*Looks around*) What a splendid apartment you have!

ATUYEVA.   Yes, a splendid, splendid apartment. What taste he has! In everything . . . in everything . . .

LIDOCHKA.   A perfectly lovely place!

KRECHINSKY.   For me, mesdames, the place has only now become lovely. (*Kisses Lidochka's hand*)

ATUYEVA.   How charming his repartee! And what a charming man! . . . There's one thing I regret, Mikhail Vasilich.

KRECHINSKY.   And what might that be, Anna Antonovna?

ATUYEVA.   That I'm not young any more. I would have fallen in love with you. Really, I would.

KRECHINSKY.   The regrets should all be mine . . . that I am not yet old.

LIDOCHKA.   That's not much of a compliment to me.

ATUYEVA.   Lidochka, you aren't jealous?

KRECHINSKY.   (*Kisses Lidochka's hand*) It is because you are jealous that I kiss your hand. But you are being unjust.

LIDOCHKA.   Why unjust?

KRECHINSKY.   I said that the regrets should be mine, but there is a vast difference between what should be and what is.

LIDOCHKA.   (*Walks over to one side of the stage and mo-*

tions to Krechinsky) Mikhail Vasilich . . . Michel . . . A word with you.

KRECHINSKY. *(Joins her)* What is it?

LIDOCHKA. A secret. *(Leads him further away from everybody)* Do you love me?

KRECHINSKY. I do.

LIDOCHKA. Very much?

KRECHINSKY. Very much.

LIDOCHKA. Michel, listen, I want you to love me terribly . . . beyond measure, beyond reason . . . *(undertone)* as I love you.

KRECHINSKY. *(Takes both her hands in his)* With all my heart and soul!

LIDOCHKA. No, only with your heart!

KRECHINSKY. *(Aside)* She'll make a sweet little wench!

ATUYEVA. *(Stealing up to them)* What's this conference about?

LIDOCHKA. Oh, just a matter of business.

ATUYEVA. The wedding dress, I wager.

LIDOCHKA. You've lost, auntie.

ATUYEVA. Then what?

KRECHINSKY. *(Pointing at his heart)* That which is under the wedding dress, Anna Antonovna.

ATUYEVA. Under the dress? *(Takes Lidochka aside)* How could you—discuss your underwear with him?

LIDOCHKA. *(Laughs)* No, auntie . . . not underwear. *(Whispers in her ear)*

KRECHINSKY. *(Runs across the stage to Muromsky)* Why don't you sit down, Piotr Konstantinych? Be so kind! Would you like a chair with a high back or a low back? *(To Raspluyev)* Chairs, Ivan Antonich, chairs. *(Raspluyev brings chairs)*

MUROMSKY. No, thank you. I'll take the sofa. More comfortable. *(Sits down)*

KRECHINSKY. Allow me to introduce a dear friend and neighbor, Ivan Antonovich Raspluyev.

RASPLUYEV.	(*Leaves the chairs, bows. Flustered*) Honored . . . honored . . . Much . . .
MUROMSKY.	(*Rising*) It is a pleasure. (*Shakes hands with Raspluyev and returns to his seat. Raspluyev moves up a chair and sits on the very edge, facing Muromsky. Krechinsky rejoins the ladies on the other side of the stage. Tea is served. Silence*)
MUROMSKY.	(*Taking a cup*) May I ask, are you in the military or civil service?
RASPLUYEV.	(*Taking a cup*) In the civ . . . civ . . . the mili . . . oh, no, in the civil service. Yes, the civil!
MUROMSKY.	Do you live in Moscow, sir, or in the countryside?
RASPLUYEV.	In Moscow, sir, in Moscow. That is, from time to time. But mostly I live in the country.
MUROMSKY.	And would you tell me, sir, where your estate is?
RASPLUYEV.	In the province of Simbirsk. Yes, Simbirsk.
MUROMSKY.	What district?
RASPLUYEV.	District, you say?
MUROMSKY.	(*Nodding*) Yes, district.
RASPLUYEV.	Oh, so you mean district! Of course, of course . . . (*Leans forward and thinks*) The district of . . . er . . . It's on the tip of my tongue . . . (*Aside*) I don't know the name of a single district in that Godforsaken wilderness. (*Aloud and snapping his fingers*) I nearly had it a moment ago, but it slipped off my tongue. Oh, Lord! . . . Mikhail Vasilich, please, what's the name of the district?
KRECHINSKY.	Which district?
RASPLUYEV.	Ours. Our district.
KRECHINSKY.	Oh, ours! It's the Ardatov district.
RASPLUYEV.	(*With a gesture to Muromsky*) That's it!
MUROMSKY.	Ardatov?

RASPLUYEV.	(*Sips his tea and nods affirmatively*) The province of Simbirsk, Ardatov district.
MUROMSKY.	But the Ardatov district is in the province of Nizhni-Novgorod.
RASPLUYEV.	(*Spluttering in his tea cup*) Nizhni-Novgorod? How did it get there? (*Laughs*) Mikhail Vasilich, please, how can this be? They say that the Ardatov district is in the province of Nizhni-Novgorod (*giggles*).
KRECHINSKY.	(*Impatiently*) Nothing wrong with that. There are two Ardatov districts. One in Nizhni-Novgorod, the other in Simbirsk.
RASPLUYEV.	(*With a gesture to Muromsky*) There you are!
MUROMSKY.	(*Also gestures*) You are quite right. There is one Ardatov in Simbirsk and another in Nizhni-Novgorod.
RASPLUYEV.	(*Also gestures*) One Ardatov in Nizhni-Novgorod, the other in Simbirsk (*pulls himself together*).
MUROMSKY.	Sorry, sir, sorry, you were right. (*Pause*) And, would you kindly tell me, who is the governor?
RASPLUYEV.	Eh? (*Aside*) What does this fool want from me? What will it lead to? (*With a gesture of desperation*) Come what may! His name is Brevnov.
MUROMSKY.	What was that?
RASPLUYEV.	Brr-revnov, sir!
MUROMSKY.	Never heard of him. Never had the honor of meeting him.
RASPLUYEV.	(*Aside*) I should think you haven't!
MUROMSKY.	Is he a good man?
RASPLUYEV.	A most worthy man. Wouldn't hurt a fly.
MUROMSKY.	A rare thing these days.
RASPLUYEV.	Hm . . . Rare? That's where you're wrong, Piotr Konstantinych. I can swear such people don't exist these days.
MUROMSKY.	But surely . . .

RASPLUYEV.   (*Heatedly*) I assure, sir, not one! Just try and find one!

MUROMSKY.   (*With sympathy*) You've had a lot of trouble in your day, it seems.

RASPLUYEV.   And so I have. (*Smoothing his coat*) Such trouble, such vexations, let me tell you, that anyone else would have come apart at the seams, but here I am—alive and all in one piece.

MUROMSKY.   (*With a sigh*) How life plays with us all . . . (*Pause*) And what kind of land do you have on your estate?

RASPLUYEV.   Land? We can't complain.

MUROMSKY.   You surely have black soil in your province? Yes, of course, that whole area is black soil.

RASPLUYEV.   Yes, yes, of course. Black soil . . . remarkably black . . . black as black can be.

MUROMSKY.   And the crops must be excellent?

RASPLUYEV.   Crops? Why, the wheat grows so thick in that backwood, I can't harvest it all (*laughs*). Believe me, I can't.

MUROMSKY.   Is that a fact?

RASPLUYEV.   Really, I can't! But who the devil cares? I don't give a hoot about it (*laughs*).

MUROMSKY.   (*Also laughs*) There's a black soil landowner for you! Tell me, how do you go about the threshing?

RASPLUYEV.   (*Aside*) He is doing this on purpose! (*Lifts his eyes heavenward*) Lord, what will it lead to? (*Wipes perspiration from his face*) About the threshing . . . this, you see . . . I can't tell you much . . . because . . .

KRECHINSKY.   (*Turning toward them*) For heaven's sake, Piotr Konstantinych, why ask him about such things. He never goes near a field except with his hunting dogs. Farming is a closed book to him.

MUROMSKY. Tell me, Mikhail Vasilich, your estate, you say, is in the Simbirsk province, but your relatives live in western Russia?

KRECHINSKY. Perfectly true. The Simbirsk estate was my mother's.

MUROMSKY. I see. And what was your mother's maiden name?

KRECHINSKY. (*Drawling*) Kolkhovskaya.

MUROMSKY. Ah, an old distinguished family.

KRECHINSKY. (*Pointing*) There is a portrait of my grandfather, my mother's father, that is.

MUROMSKY. (*Studying the portrait*) Yes, yes, I see.

KRECHINSKY. (*Pointing at Raspluyev*) This gentleman knew him. They were neighbors. (*Winks at Raspluyev and leads the ladies off stage through a side door*)

SCENE IV

Raspluyev and Muromsky

RASPLUYEV. Why, yes . . . of course . . . when I was a little boy . . . I can see him now . . . a kind gentleman, a grand old man . . . stout as you see him there . . . the portrait is a perfect likeness . . . (*Sighs*)

MUROMSKY. Is he dead?

RASPLUYEV. What in the world! . . . He (*points at the portrait*) . . . he's been dead many a year.

MUROMSKY. (*After a pause*) No, my dear sir, you try and run an estate in my province—you'd sing a different tune, I wager. We need the help of agronomy at every step. We can't do a thing without agronomy.

RASPLUYEV. You don't mean it . . . Not one step without agronomy?

MUROMSKY.	Judge for yourself. Our soil is white, cold. It won't yield anything without fertilizer.
RASPLUYEV.	(*Enjoying the turn in the conversation*) Won't yield anything? What does your soil think she is?
MUROMSKY.	Just as I said. No yield. So we simply have to try all sorts of improvements, subscribe to agricultural magazines . . . The other day I read that the English gather crops even bigger than yours.
RASPLUYEV.	(*Excited*) The English! (*Giggles*) Impossible! Wherever did you read that? What sort of agronomy can the English possibly have? They're all starving to death—that's their agronomy! I hate that nation, sir! . . .
MUROMSKY.	You can't mean it.
RASPLUYEV.	The very thought of them gives me the shudders. Imagine! Every man-jack of them is instructed in boxing. Do you, sir, know what boxing is?
MUROMSKY.	No, I don't know.
RASPLUYEV.	But I know very well . . . Let me tell you, the English have no morals . . . no love for their fellow men . . . Hm . . hm . . no! They learn this (*demonstration*) before they learn to walk. Then how can they love their fellow men? (*Straightens his coat*) No, sir, there's no love in England. But, then, one has to make allowances for them. They got that way because they're so crowded, packed in like sardines. Not a square yard of land per man. No wonder they keep bashing each other in the teeth!
MUROMSKY.	But look at all their inventions: factories, machines, ships . . .
RASPLUYEV.	You're wrong, sir, it's hunger driving them, hunger. Men will do anything if they're hungry

enough. Take any fool, if you please, lock him up in an empty closet and starve him thoroughly —the tricks he'll invent! Piotr Konstantinych, judge for yourself, but impartially, yes, impartially. The stuff we feed cows, they, the English, put in their soup! I swear to God! These days it is . . .

SCENE V

Enter Nelkin, very upset. Walks in quickly and looks about him.

MUROMSKY.   Welcome, Vladimir Dmitrich, my good friend. You've come at last. (*To Raspluyev*) Allow me to introduce you—my good neighbor and friend of the family, Vladimir Dmitrich Nelkin. (*To Nelkin*) Ivan Antonich Raspluyev. (*They bow to each other*)

RASPLUYEV.   I've had the honor.

NELKIN.   I, too, have had the honor.

MUROMSKY.   Why so late, my good friend?

NELKIN.   I was detained on business.

MUROMSKY.   Good Lord! What business can there be at this hour?

NELKIN.   Such business, Piotr Konstantinych, that it burns (*looks about him*), it scorches—that's the kind of business it is!

RASPLUYEV.   You are a man of business, I see. They all are alike: pure quicksilver.

MUROMSKY.   You ought to hear Ivan Antonich blasting the English.

RASPLUYEV.   A venomous nation, sir, venomous. Nothing honorable about them.

NELKIN.   You? You think that?

RASPLUYEV.   (*Blithely*) I do, I do.

NELKIN.   (*Laughs*)

RASPLUYEV.   (*Joins in*) Ha, ha, ha, ha! I do . . . I do . . . Ha, ha, ha.

NELKIN.   What is your name?

RASPLUYEV.   Ivan Antonich.

NELKIN.   Your last name?

RASPLUYEV.   Raspluyev.

NELKIN.   (*Buttonholes him*) Tell me, Mr. Raspluyev, where is there no evil? Is there such a place?

RASPLUYEV.   Oh, no, sir, I disagree. Evil must be weeded out, it must—root and branch.

NELKIN.   (*Paying no attention*) What is evil, where does it hide—that is the question. Take, for example, baseness and thievery in homespun, in the threadbare jacket of a starveling clerk—they're pitiful, loathsome, but not dangerous. It's frightening when baseness is all decked out in tails . . . in white gloves . . . living off someone else . . . riding about on thoroughbreds, moving in polite society, worming its way into honest houses . . . mocking honor . . . serenity . . . everything! This is what is frightening!

RASPLUYEV.   How right you are! Truly, Piotr Konstantinych, it's as bad as he says, evil is quite a common thing, I assure you. Here's one case, for ex-example . . .

NELKIN.   There are plenty of cases! That's what's so frightening! Not surprising to find a filthy shirt under a threadbare jacket. But, when a frock coat (*points at Raspluyev's*) hides a filth-ridden shirt . . .

RASPLUYEV.   (*Aside*) What's he driving at? Why harp on my coat? (*Straightens the coat in some embarrassment*) And let me tell you . . . how often some upstart comes along and pulls the wool over our eyes. A convict, sir, escapes, flies to us like a bird of passage . . . And would you believe it? He struts and puts on airs . . .

NELKIN. *(Looking him full in the face)* Puts on airs?

RASPLUYEV. Yes, sir.

NELKIN. *(Pointing at him)* A scoundrel gives himself airs. *(Laughs)*

MUROMSKY. *(Joins laughter)*

RASPLUYEV. *(Makes an attempt to laugh)* Yes, imagine, a scoundrel, and all of a sudden gives himself airs —isn't that a riot? *(Aside, grinding his teeth)* Laugh, damn you, may it choke you!

NELKIN. *(Stressing every syllable)* Yes, it's only too common. *(To Muromsky)* But it's even more appalling, Piotr Konstantinych, when our own Russian good-for-nothings, like infidels, rob and plunder their own brothers.

MUROMSKY. You've really got them on the hook!

NELKIN. *(Aside)* What's the matter with him? He's blind, blind as a bat! What shall I do? *(To Muromsky, firmly)* I must have a word with you, sir.

MUROMSKY. *(Rises)* What is it? *(Goes off to the side)*

NELKIN. Where are you?

MUROMSKY. What? I don't quite hear you.

NELKIN. I'm asking you, where are you?

MUROMSKY. What do you mean, where am I? I'm here, right here.

NELKIN. Where is here?

MUROMSKY. *(Losing his temper)* Damn it, here! Here, I say! What's eating you? Don't you know this is the home of Krechinsky? Of Mikhail Vasilich? Well? . . .

NELKIN. You are in a den of thieves.

MUROMSKY. What the devil! You're out of your mind . . . mad!

NELKIN.   It's not that I've gone mad—you've gone blind.
They are stealing your daughter from you. Can't
you see?

MUROMSKY.   (*Takes him further aside*) Listen to me, Vladimir Dmitrich, you can't say such things. You're
talking about my future son-in-law. Come to
your senses.

NELKIN.   You come to your senses, sir! You stand on the
brink of disaster . . . Look around you: you're
being taken in. They are stealing your daughter! . . A snake is coiled in your honest home, a
cardsharper, a bankrupt swindler, and thief!

RASPLUYEV.   (*Pricking up his ears*) Swindler? Thief? Could
he mean us?

MUROMSKY.   You've gone too far, sir. You have no right . . .

NELKIN.   I do have the right! Listen to me.

MUROMSKY.   What is it?

NELKIN.   Where is your diamond solitaire?

MUROMSKY.   Solitaire? You mean Lidochka's pin?

NELKIN.   Precisely.

MUROMSKY.   She has it.

NELKIN.   Are you sure?

MUROMSKY.   I'm sure.

NELKIN.   Your daughter does not have the solitaire.

MUROMSKY.   There you are—a lie!

NELKIN.   Wait, Piotr Konstantinych, wait. I'm telling
you, the solitaire is not in your house. Someone
else has it.

MUROMSKY.   Where is it?

NELKIN.   In a pawnshop.

MUROMSKY.   Rubbish! I saw it only yesterday.

NELKIN.   Yesterday is not today.

MUROMSKY.   Look here, Vladimir Dmitrich . . .

NELKIN.   (*Interrupting*) I'm telling you, Krechinsky has
pawned it. It is in the hands of a moneylender.

RASPLUYEV.   (*Eavesdropping*) Something's gone haywire . . .
I must warn him. (*Exit*)

MUROMSKY.	How did the solitaire get into Krechinsky's hands?
NELKIN.	Didn't you know he took it this morning?
MUROMSKY.	Took it? What do you mean?
NELKIN.	He . . . (*points at Raspluyev*) he called for it.
MUROMSKY.	Who? Raspluyev?
NELKIN.	Yes, Raspluyev.
MUROMSKY.	How did this happen?
NELKIN.	I called at your home this morning, and he was already there, sitting with Anna Antonovna. Just then Lidya brought in the pin. It gave me a jolt. Bah! I thought to myself, there's something fishy about his taking such a thing—I, for one, wouldn't even touch it . . . But he drove off with it . . . I followed him . . . here . . . there . . . all over town and ended up here . . .
MUROMSKY.	What did you find out?
NELKIN.	That's precisely what I'm trying to tell you! He pawned it with Bek the moneylender.
MUROMSKY.	Impossible! It just doesn't sound right.
NELKIN.	I left him but a minute ago.
MUROMSKY.	The moneylender?
NELKIN.	Yes, the moneylender. If you like, let's go and have a talk with him. He'll tell you all about it.
MUROMSKY.	(*Bewildered*) What does it mean? God Almighty, what does it all mean? Lida! Lida! Lidochka!
LIDOCHKA.	(*Runs in from the next room with a billiard cue in her hand*) Papà, papà, what is it?
MUROMSKY.	Come here. (*Undertone*) Tell me, Lidochka, your diamond solitaire . . . is it safe?
LIDOCHKA.	Safe, papà, of course, it's safe! Papà, how could you tear me away from my game? I'm playing with Michel, and he's letting me win all the time. It's such fun . . . heavenly!
NELKIN.	You are mistaken, Lidya Petrovna, your solitaire is gone.

LIDOCHKA.	What do you mean—gone?
NELKIN.	You gave it to him.
LIDOCHKA.	What if I did? (*Looks at him with amazement*) I sent it to Michel this morning, papà. He had a wager about it.
MUROMSKY.	What?
LIDOCHKA.	He had a wager with Prince Belsky . . . about the number of carats or something like that.
NELKIN.	(*To Muromsky*) A lie!
LIDOCHKA.	For heaven's sake! He has it. Only a minute ago he mentioned that he has it.
MUROMSKY.	(*Worriedly*) Well? . . .
LIDOCHKA.	So why worry, papà? He'll give it back to me.
NELKIN.	I doubt it.
LIDOCHKA.	(*Flaring up*) What are you saying? How dare you, sir?
NELKIN.	I beg you, Lidya Petrovna, don't be angry with me. What am I to do? Is it my fault? I'm ready to die for you . . . to bear torture . . . But I must . . . on my honor, I must! . .
LIDOCHKA.	(*Frightened*) God, my God! What does it mean? Papà, papà, I am frightened! (*Clings to Muromsky*) Papà dear . . .
MUROMSKY.	Don't worry, my child! Don't worry. I, myself, don't know what it means . . .

SCENE VI

Enter Atuyeva followed by Krechinsky and Raspluyev.

ATUYEVA.	What's wrong, Lidochka? What's the matter with you? Ah! It's you again, Mr. Nelkin! What tales are you spinning now? What dirt are you tracking in this time? More of your gossip and yarns?

	(Pause. General embarrassment. Krechinsky watches everyone attentively)
MUROMSKY.	*(Haltingly)* Please, Mikhail Vasilich . . . you know . . . we'd like to . . . have a family talk, just for a few minutes.
KRECHINSKY.	A family talk? Why not? I am not exactly a stranger to your family.
MUROMSKY.	Yes, of course, only . . . would you excuse us?
NELKIN.	Why beat around the bush, Piotr Konstantinych? Let's have it out. My dear sir, we're talking about the solitaire.
KRECHINSKY.	What solitaire, Piotr Konstantinych?
MUROMSKY.	You know, the one you had redone into a pin. This morning . . . you took it from my daughter?
KRECHINSKY.	Yes, I took it. Didn't she tell you I took it?
MUROMSKY.	Well, do you still have it, or don't you?
KRECHINSKY.	Aha . . . So this is . . . *(Looks at everyone in turn. A long stare at Nelkin. Addressing Muromsky)* So this is what it's all about! Tell me, where am I? In what company? Tell me, what fool, what liar, what good-for-nothing . . . *(general consternation)* has dared . . . *(Nelkin makes a threatening movement toward Krechinsky. Atuyeva holds him back)* One more step, and I'll bash your head in!
NELKIN.	*(Shouts)* No, I'll bash yours in!
KRECHINSKY.	*(Makes a rapid movement toward Nelkin, suddenly halts. His voice trembles)* Piotr Konstantinych . . . Lidochka's solitaire is here . . . Do you understand? I tell you, it's here!
MUROMSKY.	I never thought otherwise. But then he came in saying that I'm ruining my own daughter, that you are deceiving us, that you took the solitaire and pawned it. There . . . Judge for yourself . . .
KRECHINSKY.	So-o-o . . . I see it all now. But suppose he lied. Suppose he, the damn . . . forgive my language

. . . has told you a most damnable lie? What then? (*Muromsky makes a helpless gesture*) Then, I demand . . . you hear me? I demand that you take him by the collar and throw him out of the house! Do you give me your word? Do you? . . . Then take it. (*Gets the pin from his bureau*) Take it! (*Hands the pin to Lidochka, and extends his other hand to Muromsky*) Piotr Konstantinych, the next move is yours.

LIDOCHKA. (*Pushes the pin away*) No! I don't want it . . . (*Atuyeva takes the pin. Everyone gathers round her. General confusion and noise. Everyone talks at the same time*)

NELKIN. What? It's impossible! I'm telling you, it's impossible!

ATUYEVA (*Displaying the pin*) But here it is! Look at it. Here it is!

KRECHINSKY. (*To Muromsky*) It's your move, Piotr Konstantinych. I insist! I demand!

MUROMSKY. (*Completely at a loss, spreads out his arms*) I'll try. (*To Nelkin*) You see, sir, what comes of lying. (*Looks at the pin*) No doubt about it— our solitaire.

NELKIN. (*As though waking from a bad dream*) Merciful God! Where am I? What kind of a trick is this? (*Goes up to Lidochka, tugs at her sleeve*) Lidya Petrovna, let me explain . . .

KRECHINSKY. Get away from her! (*Brushing her sleeve*) Take your dirty hands off!

NELKIN. (*Buries his head in his hands*) My God! What does it all mean, my God?!

MUROMSKY. (*To Nelkin*) Wherever did you hear that nonsense? From whom?

KRECHINSKY. (*Interrupting*) Let me handle it. Questions are out of place now. Polite conversation is finished.

	We are now dealing with facts, not hearsay. Is this your pin?
MUROMSKY.	Yes.
KRECHINSKY.	(*To Nelkin, pointing to the door*) Get out!
MUROMSKY.	There's nothing for you to do here now. You'd better go.
NELKIN.	(*Takes his hat and walks up to Krechinsky*) I'm prepared to give you satisfaction . . . (*Krechinsky points to the door. Nelkin comes up to him and shouts*) This very minute . . . to the death!
	(*Confusion. Muromsky, Lidochka, Atuyeva, Raspluyev surround Krechinsky. Nelkin stands alone. All speak almost simultaneously*)
LIDOCHKA.	No, no never! I won't allow it. (*To Nelkin*) Go away! Go!
ATUYEVA.	Go away. God be with you, go away.
MUROMSKY.	Enough, gentlemen, I beg you!
KRECHINSKY.	(*Stepping out of the group*) So-o-o! (*Assumes a theatrical pose*) So that's what you want! Satisfaction! What satisfaction, may I ask? (*Scornfully*) You want to shoot it out? . . . (*Laughs*) I should put a pistol in your hand and offer myself as a target . . . On second thought, fine. But on the condition that I spit in your eyes for every shot you fire. Those are my conditions. Even tomorrow, if you wish. But right now . . . hey, servants!
RASPLUYEV.	Hey, servants! That's the way to handle him! (*Enter Fyodor and two servants*)
KRECHINSKY.	Take him by the scruff of the neck and throw him out.
NELKIN.	God in heaven! Is this a dream? A nightmare? (*Pinches himself. Bitterly*) Truth, truth, where is your power? (*Leaves in a daze*)

RASPLUYEV. (*Bolts the door behind him*) Adieu! (*Giggles*) Go and look for it. (*Aside*) Judge for yourself. The search for truth is the shortest way to the poorhouse. Go ahead, look for it, brother, you're still young, keep looking . . .
(*Long pause. Muromsky still disturbed. Lidochka stands motionless. Atuyeva looks angrily at Muromsky*)

SCENE VII

KRECHINSKY. (*After a silence*) Well, Piotr Konstantinych, are you satisfied?

MUROMSKY. Completely satisfied, completely . . . He must have gone mad.

KRECHINSKY. I, too, am perfectly satisfied. And now we can make an end to it all.

MUROMSKY. (*Perplexed*) An end? How?

KRECHINSKY. The usual way. There's been an ugly incident. You yourself blackened my good name. With such a stain, what kind of a husband would I make for your daughter? Piotr Konstantinych, I must release you from your consent, and you, Lidochka, to you I return your heart. Take it back, be happy . . . forget me.

LIDOCHKA. What are you trying to say, Michel? What are you saying? I don't understand you. Hearts are not made to be given back. My heart is yours! Papà, why don't you say something?! For God's sake, why don't you say something! It's our fault. (*In despair*) Papà, it's all our fault!

MUROMSKY. (*Hastily*) Yes, yes . . . how can you, have mercy, Mikhail Vasilich. I never . . . He's a real half-wit. How can you take him seriously?

KRECHINSKY.	And what about your own behavior? If this windbag was able to insult me, just think how you yourself have offended me. Tomorrow, someone else may come along and say that I am a cardsharper, a swindler, and you will take it all in and start inquiries.
MUROMSKY.	Mikhail Vasilich, how can you?
KRECHINSKY.	I know something about middle-class morality. But I want you to know that my pride will not permit me to accept its dictates. I either trust a man, or I do not. There is no middle course. I don't need your diamond solitaires, or your money! If anyone ever mentions your money to me, I'll ram it down his throat!
LIDOCHKA.	(*Seizes his hand*) Michel, please! If you still love me even a little . . .
MUROMSKY.	Mikhail Vasilich, I beg you, forgive me. Forgive me, I beg you . . .
KRECHINSKY.	(*Thinks of something. Aside*) That madman has gone straight to Bek . . .
LIDOCHKA.	You're saying nothing? You are offended? I know, there is neither forgiveness nor pity in your heart . . . What do you want us to do? We will do anything . . .
KRECHINSKY.	(*Takes her by both hands with emotion*) Oh, Lidochka, what a heart you have—what a good heart! Am I worthy of it?
LIDOCHKA.	You're mocking me, Michel . . .
KRECHINSKY.	Well, Piotr Konstantinych, your hand!
MUROMSKY.	At last! (*Shakes hands*) At long last!
KRECHINSKY.	I'll tell you what. We'll celebrate the wedding tomorrow, to put an end to all gossip.
MUROMSKY.	Let it be tomorrow.
KRECHINSKY.	And after the wedding we'll go straight to the country.
MUROMSKY.	To the country.

KRECHINSKY. And you'll never let Nelkin set foot in your house again.

MUROMSKY. The devil take him. What do I want with him now?

KRECHINSKY. You promise . . . on your honor?

MUROMSKY. Anything you want. I agree to everything. My head is swimming. (*Gesture*) There is only one . . . she (*voice breaks*) . . . my only . . .

KRECHINSKY. (*Looks at his watch*) Already ten o'clock! Time for you to go home Lidochka. You're still upset . . .

LIDOCHKA. No, not at all! (*Takes his hand*) You have forgiven? . . Haven't you? Say yes.

KRECHINSKY. Yes, a hundred times yes. All is forgotten, except . . . except that you belong to me. Tomorrow you will be my property . . . you'll be mine.

LIDOCHKA. Yes, Michel, yours . . . all yours. Tell me again you love me.

KRECHINSKY. (*Studying her*) Do you doubt it?

LIDOCHKA. It isn't that . . . I want to hear that word once more. There is something special in that word . . . Something . . . I don't know what . . . a kind of fear and pain.

KRECHINSKY. (*Uneasily*) Pain? How so?

LIDOCHKA. Don't be alarmed. I wouldn't exchange this pain for all the joys in the world. Now tell me: do you love me?

KRECHINSKY. (*Whispers*) I love you.

LIDOCHKA. (*Takes him by one hand and covers her eyes with the other*) You know, Michel, this moment my heart froze . . . it stopped beating . . . Tell me, is this love?

KRECHINSKY. No, my angel, it is only one half of love.

LIDOCHKA. (*Smiling*) Only half? . . . What a cheat you are . . . when I am already prepared to give everything for it . . . (*Krechinsky kisses her hand*) Yes, everything, everything! (*Whispers*) The whole world.

KRECHINSKY. (*Kisses her hand again, speaks to Muromsky*) Well, Piotr Konstantinych, it's time you were going home.

MUROMSKY. Fine, we are ready . . .

KRECHINSKY. Yes, do go home and send Lidochka straight to bed. She must have a good rest. Tomorrow, Lidochka, you shall be fresh, rosy-cheeked and pretty as befits a bride. (*Stops to think for a moment*) Or no, I'd better take you home myself and see to everything.

(*Muromsky, Atuyeva, and Lidochka getting ready to leave*)

RASPLUYEV. (*To Krechinsky*) You're quite right, you'd better see to everything yourself.

KRECHINSKY. (*Takes Raspluyev aside*) Don't you leave this place. If that fellow Nelkin comes barging in again, let him in and keep him here even if you have to knock him down with the poker. Don't let him go until I come back. Get it?

RASPLUYEV. Don't worry, don't worry. I'll tree that bear.

KRECHINSKY. And from that point on, everything is under control. The Muromsky house will be closed to him, I'll see to that. He won't worm his way in there.

MUROMSKY. Well, Mikhail Vasilich, let's go, we are ready.

KRECHINSKY. Let's go, let's go. (*Picks up his hat quickly. The doorbell rings abruptly. Everyone stops in his tracks*) Eh? What? Who is it? (*Shouts*) Hey, there! Fyodor! Don't let anyone in . . . not a soul! (*Noises. Another ring. Voices*) So-o-o . . . This is it! (*Enter Fyodor*) What happened? Who's there?

FYODOR. Mr. Nelkin. He's brought some people with him, and all shouting to open the door. (*Voices:*

"Open the door, open the door!" *The bell rings insistently*)

KRECHINSKY. (*Furious*) So, he wants me to kill him on the spot! (*Breaks the arm off a chair. Muromsky and Lidochka seize him by the hand*)

LIDOCHKA. Michel! Michel!

MUROMSKY. In the name of heaven, calm down! What has come over you? (*They all surround him*)

KRECHINSKY. Go chase him away!

RASPLUYEV. (*Runs to the door*) Right away. (*Returns on the run*) But there's a whole mob . . . at least five of them.

KRECHINSKY. Go back! Die, but throw them out!

RASPLUYEV. Die, die! Have a heart, Mikhail Vasilich. It isn't such a trifling matter, to die. (*The noise grows. Voices:* "Open the door! Break it down!")

KRECHINSKY. (*Breaks away from Muromsky and Lidochka, runs to the door*) Let me go! I must put a stop to it myself. (*Gritting his teeth*) I'll kill him . . . the dog.

FYODOR. (*Enters*) The police are here, master. They order us to open the door.

KRECHINSKY. (*Loses all self-control*) Don't move! Don't open the door! I'll bash the brains out of anyone who moves! . . (*Brandishes the arm of the chair. Suddenly stops*) The police! . . . (*Dull tone*) Aa . . . (*Throws the chair arm into a corner*) The game is up! . . . (*Walks to the side*) Open the door. (*Noises, sound of door being opened*)

SCENE VIII

Nelkin rushes into the room and runs straight up to Lidochka. Bek runs in after him. His eyes dart about until he spots Krechinsky.

Runs toward him and plants himself in front of Krechinsky, to block escape. A police officer appears in the doorway.

BEK.   Here he is, the thief! The robber! He pawned a piece of glass. Took my good money for a piece of glass, the robber! (*Runs about the stage in excitement. Krechinsky stands calmly, his arms folded*) Take him! Here he is, take him!

LIDOCHKA.   (*Screams in anguish*)
(*Nelkin, Muromsky, and Atuyeva run up to her. Krechinsky, too, makes a move toward her*)

BEK.   Don't move! Don't move, swindler! Robber!

RASPLUYEV.   (*Hides behind Krechinsky's back*)

POLICE OFFICER.   (*To Bek*) Calm down, please, calm yourself. (*To Krechinsky*) Permit me to ask your name and surname.

KRECHINSKY.   Mikhail Vasilich Krechinsky.

POLICE OFFICER.   (*To Raspluyev*) Your name and surname, please?

RASPLUYEV.   (*In a panic*) Mik . . . Mikh . . . ail Vas . . silich . . . what . . . what . . . shall I do? (*Krechinsky silently looks him in the eye*) I . . . I . . . I have no . . . no name. That's the way I am . . . without a name.

POLICE OFFICER.   I am asking you: what is your name and surname?

RASPLUYEV.   But how can I tell you if I have no name?

KRECHINSKY.   (*Calmly*) His name is Ivan Antonich Raspluyev.
(*The police officer makes a note, joins the other group, and talks quietly to Muromsky almost to the end of the play. Krechinsky makes a sudden movement*)

BEK.   (*Shouts*) Don't move! Don't move! Hold him! Hold him! (*Stands in Krechinsky's path, his arms outspread*)

POLICE OFFICER. Be calm, please. I beg you, be calm.

BEK. (*At the top of his voice*) Hold him, the beast! He's a wild beast. He'll get away. He took six thousand rubles for a piece of glass . . . for a cheap imitation! It's forgery! Arrest him! Put him in jail!

LIDOCHKA. (*Detaches herself from the group and walks up to Bek*) Sir, please, sir. Let him go. Here is the pin . . . the one that should have been pawned . . . Take it . . . it was . . . (*bursts into tears*) it was all a mistake!

MUROMSKY and ATUYEVA. Lidochka! What are you doing, Lidochka!

BEK. Eh? What's this, little lady? (*Looks at the pin*) The pin! The real one! Dear Lord! What a girl! Heavenly kindness . . . Angelic meekness . . .

LIDOCHKA. (*Sobs, her face buried in her hands*)

KRECHINSKY. (*Aside, facing the audience*) What a relief! (*Mops his forehead*) A woman again . . .

ATUYEVA. Piotr Konstantinych, what are we to do now?

MUROMSKY. Run! Run from here! Run from disgrace! (*Lidochka runs headlong off the stage, followed by Nelkin, Muromsky, and Atuyeva*)

Curtain